THE DEPARTMENTAL GUIDE AND RECORD BOOK FOR STUDENT OUTCOMES ASSESSMENT AND INSTITUTIONAL EFFECTIVENESS

By the same authors

Assessment Case Studies: Common Issues in Implementation with Various Approaches to Resolution

A Practitioner's Handbook for Institutional Effectiveness and Outcomes Assessment Implementation

The Department Head's Guide to Assessment Implementation in Administrative and Educational Support Units

THE DEPARTMENTAL GUIDE AND RECORD BOOK FOR STUDENT OUTCOMES ASSESSMENT AND INSTITUTIONAL EFFECTIVENESS

by
James O. Nichols
Director, University Planning and Institutional Research, University of Mississippi

and

Karen W. Nichols
Executive Director, Institutional Effectiveness Associates

AGATHON PRESS
New York

Library of Congress Cataloging-in Publication Data
Nichols, James O. (James Oliver), 1941-
    The departmental guide and record book for student outcomes assessment
and institutional effectiveness / by James O. Nichols and Karen W. Nichols
        p.   cm.
    "Third edition...revised updated"--Pref.
    Includes bibliographic references
        ISBN 0-87586-129-6
        1. Education, Higher—United States—Evaluation—Handbooks,
manuals, etc. 2. Universities and colleges—United States—Departments—
Evaluation—Handbooks, manuals, etc.   3. Universities and colleges—
United States—Examinations—Handbooks, manuals, etc.
    I. Nichols, Karen W. II. Title

LB2331.63.N52   2000
378.1'07—dc21   00-038624

CONTENTS

PREFACE

On any campus there are three entities involved with the implementation of institutional effectiveness or educational (student) outcomes assessment. These entities are: (a) the Chief Executive Officer, (b) the individual or group charged by the Chief Executive Officer with the responsibility for implementation, and (c) the academic and nonacademic departments where implementation will actually take place. Chief Executive Officers can reasonably (given their other responsibilities) be expected to do no more than understand the importance of institutional effectiveness or educational (student) outcomes assessment implementation, give their active support to the process, and provide the resources to see that the job gets done. The individual or group given responsibility for implementation on campus can be expected to organize and support the process. However, the majority of the actual work in implementation of institutional effectiveness or educational (student) outcomes assessment will take place within the institution's academic and nonacademic departments.

A Practitioner's Handbook for Institutional Effectiveness and Student Outcomes Assessment, now in its third edition, is intended to be a working reference for that individual or group on the campus charged by the Chief Executive Officer with responsibility for implementation of institutional effectiveness or educational (student) outcomes assessment. *A Practitioner's Handbook* (3rd ed.) provides a generic model for implementation of institutional effectiveness and educational (student) outcomes assessment as well as resource sections containing detailed information regarding essential components of the implementation process. *Assessment Case Studies* relates the manner in which eleven institutions, relatively mature in the implementation process, dealt with common issues encountered in the process from the institutional to the departmental levels. This third edition of *The Departmental Guide and Record Book,* also revised updated, is designed to assist the busy departmental administrator in leading the implementation process within the individual educational programs at the institution and recording the results of that implementation. The four publications, *A Practitioner's Handbook* (3rd ed.), *Assessment Case Studies, Assessment Implementation in Administrative and Educational Support Units,* and *The Departmental Guide* (3rd ed.), are complementary and cross-referenced for convenience.

The Departmental Guide and Record Book is not meant to be a scholarly work; references are included in only those few instances in which not to do so would border upon plagiarism. It is intended as a document that can be reviewed quickly by the reader who has little time for (or perhaps interest in) assessment theory, but is required to guide implementation within the department.

This third edition of *The Departmental Guide and Record Book* includes a number of substantive changes from earlier editions. The most noticeable is the provision of www based access to the improved assessment record book forms for academic programs and instructions for their completion described in Appendix A. However, also included in this edition are brief chapters and examples regarding assessment in General Education, as well as, graduate and professional level education and a "Dozen Questions" for evaluation of assessment activities. Absent from this edition are previously included comments and examples regarding assessment in educational support and administrative units that are now included in Assessment Implementation in Administrative and Educational Support Units.

Over the last dozen years, the authors have assisted almost 200 institutions, from major research universities to two-year colleges, in the implementation of institutional effectiveness and educational (student) outcomes assessment activities. During the course of that service, discussions with the departmental chairs have brought forth a relatively consistent series of issues or questions requiring resolution by departmental administrators in the course of implementation. This experience, actually working with departmental administrators implementing institutional effectiveness or assessment of educational (student) outcomes, has formed the basis for the material contained in *The Departmental Guide and Record Book*.

If implementation activities on campus are to be successful, there is no doubt that the Chief Executive Officer must support such action and that the individual or group charged with responsibility for the effort must function effectively. However, equally as important (many would say more important) is the role of the departmental administrator in implementation. Institutional effectiveness and educational (student) outcomes assessment is not possible on a campus without successful implementation within academic programs. *The Departmental Guide and Record Book* is intended to assist those charged with this responsibility.

James O. Nichols   Karen W. Nichols

January 1, 2000

Chapter 1

WHAT CAN BE EXPECTED FROM *THE DEPARTMENTAL GUIDE AND RECORD BOOK?*

The purpose of *The Departmental Guide and Record Book* is to provide a brief resource to explain and assist in implementation of educational (student) outcomes assessment or support of institutional effectiveness activities within the academic departments of an institution. *The Departmental Guide and Record Book* is unashamedly prescriptive in nature, suggests certain actions, provides a usable format for departmental implementation, and describes departmental implementation as part of an overall institutional program. While most readers of *The Departmental Guide* do not have time to "reinvent the assessment wheel" and hence, the "cookbook" approach offered in this publication, there is no implication that the methodology proposed herein is the only one through which successful implementation can be achieved.

As you review this document, you should make a list of points "for further clarification" or "to challenge" regarding the appropriateness of the procedures suggested for your specific department. The value of *The Departmental Guide* is not in providing a fixed set of activities for departmental implementation, but in offering a "starting place" which will raise many of the issues that must be resolved on each campus and in each department for implementation to successfully proceed. Following resolution of these issues and based upon the guidance contained in the following pages, each department's needs should be relatively self-evident.

How Does *The Departmental Guide and Record Book* Relate to *A Practitioner's Handbook for Institutional Effectiveness and Outcomes Assessment Implementation* (3rd ed.)?

The two publications are closely related. *A Practitioner's Handbook* (3rd ed.) is intended for the institutional level person or group charged by the Chief Executive Officer with coordination of overall institutional effectiveness implementation. Hence, *A Practitioner's Handbook* (3rd ed.) is longer, covers a greater breadth and depth of information providing additional references for clarification, and focuses at a different level (the institutional) than does *The Departmental Guide and Record Book*. Additionally, *A Practitioner's Handbook* (3rd ed.) is premised upon implementation of a comprehensive program of institutional effectiveness operations, which is one of several contexts within which *The Departmental Guide and Record Book* may be found useful.

While compatible with and supportive of *A Practitioner's Handbook, The Departmental Guide and Record Book* is more than a summary of the points made in *A Practitioner's Handbook* (3rd ed.). Though there is naturally a considerable overlap of subjects and examples between the publications, *The Departmental Guide* addresses these subjects from the perspective of a departmental administrator charged with implementation. It seeks to raise and, where appropriate, answers the questions which most departmental administrators pose.

Establishing a Consistent Assessment Terminology

There are enough different terms regarding assessment utilized in various portions of the country to fill several pages. *The Departmental Guide and Record Book* (2nd ed.) as well as *A Practitioner's Handbook* (3rd ed.) and *Assessment Case Studies* attempt to use a consistent set of relatively generic terms to describe activities at the institutional and departmental/program level. The most important of those terms at the departmental level are defined and described below:

- **Intended Educational Outcome**—This term describes *what the departmental faculty intend for a student to be able to think, know, or do when they've completed a given educational program.* In some portions of the country, this is known as an expected educational result, an intended student academic achievement, instructional objective, or intended student outcome. Intended educational outcomes can be assumed to be synonymous with all of these terms for the purpose of this publication.
- **Instructional Departments**—Those entities at an institution in which academic or instructional programs are housed.
- **Criteria for Program Success**—The benchmark that the department sets and against which the program's performance is judged by the faculty within the department. These criteria are most often stated in terms of percentages, percentiles, averages, or other quantitative measures.

Most of the other terms utilized in this publication are relatively well understood; however, those listed above can cause some confusion due to the use of different terminology in various portions of the country.

Determination of the Context for Implementation and Its Implications for the Department

Very seldom is a departmental administrator asked to implement educational (student) outcomes assessment in a vacuum. Determination of the context or institutional circumstances within which a department is asked to initiate assessment activities is the first priority for a departmental administrator. These contexts can be grouped into the following categories, each of which has its own implications for departmental implementation:

- Implementation of a comprehensive program of institutional effectiveness

established to meet regional or other accreditation criteria
- Response to state-mandated assessment programs for accountability to the public
- Assessment of student academic achievement for the purpose of regional or professional accreditation
- Pure/intrinsic student outcomes assessment

A Practitioner's Handbook for Institutional Effectiveness and Outcomes Assessment Implementation (3rd ed.), the publication to which this third edition of *The Departmental Guide and Record Book* is linked, is designed to facilitate implementation of a comprehensive program of institutional effectiveness operations to meet regional accreditation criteria. Figure 1, the Institutional Effectiveness Paradigm shown on the following page, illustrates this context.

In this paradigm, (a) the institution establishes an Expanded Statement of Institutional Purpose; (b) academic and nonacademic departments identify statements of Intended Educational (Instructional or Student), Research, and Public Service Outcomes and Administrative Objectives which are linked to and support this Expanded Statement of Institutional Purpose; (c) assessment of the extent to which departmental and program statements of intended outcomes or objectives are met is accomplished; (d) the results of assessment activities are utilized both to determine the extent to which departmental intentions have been met (hence, effectiveness of the institution has been demonstrated) and to improve departmental and programmatic operations. Within this context (See pages 7 through 11 of the third edition of *A Practitioner's Handbook* for a more detailed description of the Institutional Effectiveness Paradigm), the instructional departments will be expected to:

- Establish statements of intended educational outcomes that are related to or supportive of the Expanded Institutional Statement of Purpose;
- Play a major role in identification, and to varying degrees implementation, of procedures and means to assess the extent to which these intended outcomes have been accomplished; and,
- Use the results of assessment to improve student learning or departmental operations.

The type of institutional effectiveness planning needed to implement the paradigm provided in Figure 1 differs from the strategic planning often taking place on campuses. Both types of planning are necessary and often required by regional accrediting associations. However, they are different in both their substance and their approach to planning and it is important that institutions recognize and respect these differences (see Figure 2).

Strategic planning on campuses is frequently a product of presidential leadership or the requirements of the governing board. Regional accrediting associations also often require some form of strategic planning activity. Such planning focuses upon the question: "What actions can we take to implement the Expanded Statement of Purpose?" As such, strategic planning often results in a series of action plans that are frequently long-range in nature and often require additional resources to put into action the necessary processes to accomplish the statement of purpose.

On the other hand, planning to implement the institutional effectiveness para-

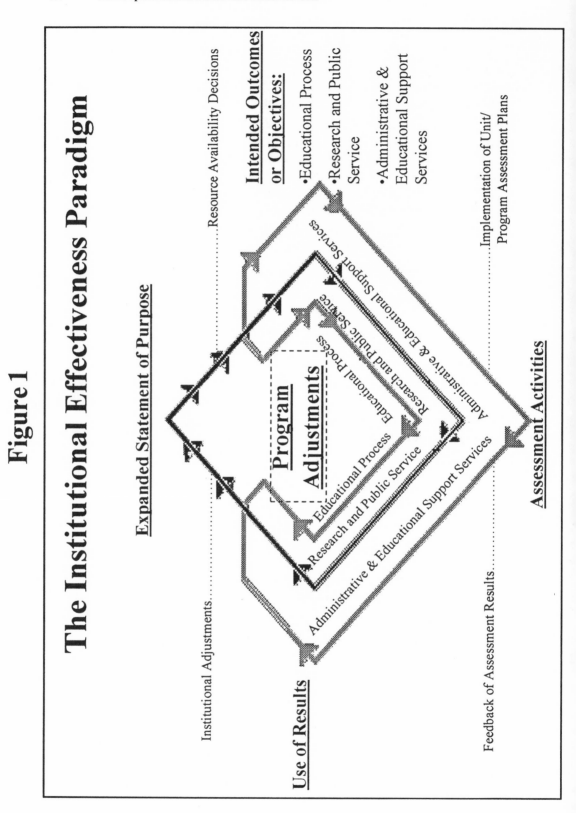

Figure 1

The Institutional Effectiveness Paradigm

digm shown in Figure 1 answers the basic question: "How well are our students learning and administrative services (AES) functioning?" Thus, institutional effectiveness planning is very ends or outcomes oriented and focuses upon the results of the institution's effort as measured by student learning in its instructional programs and services provided through its AES units. It is vital that an institution recognize that both forms of planning are necessary.

Figure 2

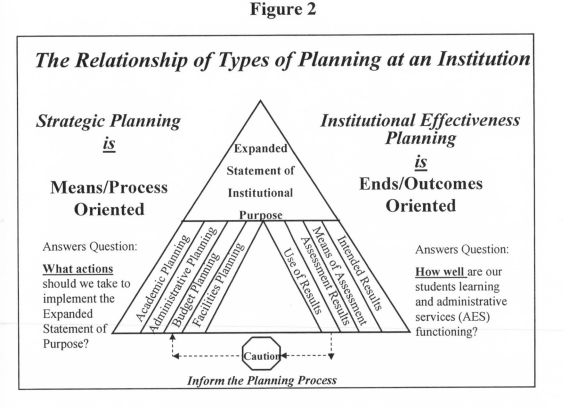

. What are the primary implications for a departmental administrator being asked to implement assessment activities as part of a comprehensive program of institutional effectiveness?

- An institutional statement of purpose exists which the department is being asked to support through establishment of statements of intended educational outcomes. This statement of institutional purpose is of vital importance in guiding departmental implementation.
- The purpose of departmental implementation is to demonstrate at that level a set of assessment procedures which the campus has relative freedom to develop, rather than to meet externally determined student performance standards.

- Other portions of the institution (including nonacademic departments) will be implementing this process concurrently and common institutional formats and means of assessment may be available to assist the department.
- The department will ultimately need to demonstrate and record its use of assessment data to improve student learning and/or its own operations.

Within this institutional effectiveness context, departmental statements of intended outcomes and assessment of their accomplishment are the **means** through which institutional effectiveness is validated. Hence, comprehensive implementation ultimately in all academic programs is essential and will be required of the institution.

To a departmental administrator, implementation of outcomes assessment as a "response to state-mandated assessment programs for accountability to the public" has a number of substantive implications.

- The purpose of implementation is to impress the public; hence, objectivity is limited, use of the resulting data for improvement of learning is often considered inconsequential, and faculty resistance is assured.
- If institutions are required to submit an assessment plan for approval and then to submit evidence of the plan's implementation, there are a number of decisions which the department needs to consider in design of the plan which will impact its usefulness on the campus.
- The use of standardized cognitive examinations will be either mandated or strongly suggested by the state as these instruments have more apparent validity with the public and will facilitate comparisons across institutions.
- Implementation in only those programs required by the state is probable; therefore, institutional support and guidance may be limited. However, pressure for impressive assessment results will be maximized.

Implementation of educational (student) outcomes assessment for accountability purposes is the most sterile, potentially prescriptive, threatening, and largely unproductive (as to impact on the institutional operations) context for implementation at the departmental level.

Some regional and professional accrediting associations require that member institutions "assess student academic achievement." This emphasis is apparently less upon demonstration of overall institutional effectiveness through assessment of departmental intended educational outcomes linked to an institutional statement of purpose than it is on assessment for improvement of student learning. Among the professional as well as regional accrediting associations, there remains the flexibility to identify means of outcome assessment and, in most cases, for the institution to set its own standards for student achievement. In some of the regional and professional accrediting associations who utilize this method, this approach appears to be at least as much focused upon the act of assessment, as on the following actions to improve student learning. What then are the implications for departments implementing assessment of student academic achievement under these conditions?

- Less tie to the institutional level is required.
- A clear understanding of the specific (professional or regional) accreditation criteria will be needed.

- Locally developed, as well as standardized means of assessment, should be considered.
- Even if not required by the accrediting agency, departments should identify intended educational outcomes to focus the assessment effort on their most important expectations and to avoid assessing only those items which are easily measurable, but which may be of little importance.

The most ideal, and least likely, circumstance under which a department will be asked to undertake implementation of educational outcomes assessment activities is that based solely on the intrinsic merit of the process. Under these circumstances, no external pressure is exerted on the institution and motivation for implementation flows from one or more individuals in the institution or potentially the department. The focus of such motivation is probably improvement of student learning. The implications of such implementation include:

- Little pressure, control, or support for the effort beyond the institution and potentially the department.
- Greater likelihood of positive faculty support and involvement.
- Shorter duration of implementation as key individuals change positions.

Each of these contexts (institutional effectiveness, state-mandated accountability, assessment of student achievement for accreditation, and implementation based upon intrinsic value) bring with it a host of implications some of which have been addressed. However, to fully understand the nuances of an individual campus's implementation, the following questions should be raised and answered:

- Why is our department being asked to implement educational outcomes assessment activities (establishment of context)?
- What specifically is expected as a result of the department's efforts and by when?
- What are other components of the institution being asked to accomplish and how should our departmental implementation relate to theirs?
- What coordination, technical expertise, and/or logistical support can the department expect from the institution's central administration?
- Is their a standardized institutional form or format for recording departmental assessment activities?

Is It a Degree Program, Major, Emphasis, or Concentration?

Most regional accrediting agencies require the establishment of statements of intended educational outcomes for academic programs at institutions. The problem is in defining what is an academic program at the institution. At public institutions, the term academic program is normally defined in terms of courses of instruction approved by a central governing board or coordinating agency and most commonly listed in a *degree program inventory* for the institution. In the case of private institutions, an academic program is normally identified as the *majors* which the institution indicates offering in its catalog. The difficulty at both public and private institutions are those groups of courses known as an "emphasis" or "concentration" within a degree program or major. The question becomes when is an "emphasis" or "concentration" an academic program? In many cases in the public sector, truly different courses of instruction have been merged under one degree program umbrella in order to insure their continuation through the maintenance of a sufficient number of graduates to avoid termination by the state agency. It is suggested that in the case of the public sector in particular, the institution begins its definition of an academic program at the degree program level and then (only when apparently needed) examine within the degree programs the nature of the course(s) of instruction actually offered under that designation. If there are substantial differences (defined as 18 unique hours to an area of study at either the graduate or undergraduate level) in the courses of instruction within a single degree program, then in essence there is a separate major or degree program in existence. Under those circumstances, separate sets of intended educational outcomes should be prepared for each of the different courses of instruction within a given degree program. Private colleges may find this approach necessary also. It should be borne in mind that the more different sets of intended educational outcomes established, the more assessment work will be necessary.

Use of *The Departmental Guide and Record Book* in Implementation

Regardless of which context for implementation is identified as being present at an institution, the departments should: (a) identify intended educational, outcomes; (b) develop, and in some cases implement, appropriate assessment procedures to determine accomplishments of their or programmatic expectations identified; and (c) be able to demonstrate use of assessment results to improve student learning or departmental operations. Chapters II and III of this *Departmental Guide* will "walk you through" many of the issues you'll face in this task and suggest common sense solutions gleaned from working with more than 300 institutions as they have implemented outcomes assessment in one context or another. It should be emphasized that there exists a logical order for implementation activities at the departmental level. That order is the **establishment of intended educational outcomes followed by the identification of appropriate means of assessment**. At many colleges, the tendency will be to "jump" to identification of the means of assessment which are tangible entities and then to "backtrack" into identification of the intended educational outcomes which those means of assessment were designed to measure. This action repeatedly results in frustration, useless expenditure of funds, and failure to utilize the results of means of assessment. Readers are urged to follow the activity shown first in Chapter II, regarding identification of intended educational outcomes and then to move to the material in Chapter III, regarding means of assessment. Chapter IV discusses "closing the loop" to demonstrate use of assessment results to improve programming, introduces the complete "five column model," and references the Assessment Record Book contained in Appendix A. Chapter VI draws together some recurring themes in closing. Take the next few hours (approximately eighty pages) to profit from the experience of others, and ease your own departmental implementation.

Chapter II

PREPARING STATEMENTS OF INTENDED EDUCATIONAL (STUDENT) OUTCOMES

What Are Statements of Intended Educational (Student) Outcomes and Why Need We Prepare Them?

Statements of intended educational (student) outcomes are descriptions of what academic departments intend for students to know (cognitive), think (attitudinal) or do (behavioral) when they have completed their degree programs, as well as their general education or "core" curricula. While some departments such as English and mathematics (due to their heavy service course commitments) will have primary interest in statements of intended educational (student) outcomes established for the general education program, most departmental attention will be focused on development of statements of intended educational outcomes for each degree program (major) in the department.

If the department is implementing assessment activities as a portion of a comprehensive program of institutional effectiveness, it will be required to establish statements of intended educational outcomes linked to and supporting the Expanded Statement of Institutional Purpose. If not, the department should establish such statements for its own use to focus the assessment effort and increase the probability of use of assessment results in a meaningful way by the faculty.

No institution or department has the resources or time to continually assess all possible aspects of each academic program. Given this limitation, priorities for the assessment effort must be set to avoid measuring the meaningless as an easy way out, or "choking to death" on an assessment effort of gargantuan size. Hence, it is logical to begin or focus the department's assessment efforts on those expectations for graduates which have been identified as of primary importance.

In the case of state assessment initiatives for accountability purposes in which even the specific assessment instrument may have been mandated, the primary challenge (other than doing well) will be developing some sense of faculty ownership and willingness to use the resulting data. By bringing forth statements of intended educational (student) outcomes in the cognitive area covered by such mandated assessment procedures, there becomes a limited departmental need for and potential use of results of such state-mandated assessment instruments.

The Nature of Statements of Intended Educational (Student) Outcomes

Results vs. Process

If you ask faculty in most academic departments "What do you do?" the majority will respond, "I teach." If you ask most departmental administrators "What does your department do?" many will respond that the department "teaches classes," "offers programs," or perhaps "conducts research." Each of these responses, while undoubtedly correct, illustrates the extent to which we in academe are focused upon the educational "process" or what we (faculty) intend to do, rather than upon what the impact or result of our actions will be on our students or clients. To use an athletic analogy, we focus on perfecting plays (classes) or a combination of plays (curricula) rather than the final score (the knowledge, attitudes, or abilities our graduates have acquired).

This traditional "process" orientation or focus within academe is frequently reflected in statements of departmental intentions which describe: "adding another course to a major," "reducing teaching loads," "improving faculty development programs," and that all-time favorite, "raising salaries to regional or national averages." As laudable as each of the above notions may be, they do not constitute statements of intended educational or student "outcomes" and should be avoided in the pursuit of institutional effectiveness. It is important to note that the establishment of intended educational (student) outcomes is most related to educational planning, rather than fiscal or resource oriented planning efforts which may be in existence at the institution.

Results-oriented statements of intended educational (student) outcomes should resemble statements describing what graduates or program completers will know (cognitive), think (attitudes), or do (behavioral/performance). In addition to this being a relatively different manner of thought for some in academe, it can be both difficult and threatening. It requires additional thought to extend our planning past what we are doing toward what the impact of this action will be. In other cases, faculty may be unable to identify a desirable intended result of their activity (teaching a particular class), but know that they enjoy teaching that class. In either case, exertion of the necessary additional thought by "screwing up one's courage" to admit that the contribution of some courses to program intended educational outcomes is not apparent must be accomplished so that statements reflecting the most important intended educational outcomes in each program can be formulated.

The Importance (?) of Stating Intended Educational (Student) Outcomes in the Correct Manner

Several times in the history of higher education, waves of behaviorism have threatened to engulf the academic enterprise in an ocean of requirements, methods, criteria, and/or specifications concerning the "correct" method for stating educational objectives in behavioral (outcomes) terms. The rejection of this misplaced emphasis on "means" and "form," coupled with a reluctance to tolerate such "educationese" by the balance of the academic community, has made the mention of (not to even think of discussion and implementation) "student outcomes" an almost blasphemous act in some liberal arts departments.

There is no "correct" means or method for stating intended educational outcomes. The only criteria of paramount importance to consider regarding the means for expressing statements of intended educational outcomes is that the statements are clear and well understood by faculty in the department. In that regard, statements emanating from the faculties in the humanities can be expected to be very different from those of the faculties in business. Those statements from fine arts faculty will be very different from engineering faculty. In all of these cases, each statement can be viewed as correct if it is clearly understood by its originators and is student (results) oriented.

If you, as a departmental administrator, focus on or are provided with a prescriptive set of requirements, specifications, or criteria for wording statements of intended educational outcomes, you can count on a high probability of failure in your implementation effort. Faculty are generally willing to discuss, debate, and work diligently on matters of substance regarding their discipline; but most have little patience with what they perceive as a misplaced emphasis upon bureaucratic procedures.

Virtually the entire effort in identification of intended educational outcomes for each degree program should be directed at the substance of those outcomes, rather than the means for their expression. This focus on substance will be more than a sufficient challenge for most faculties and if there exists an absolutely compelling reason for the standardization of expression, it can be accomplished at the institutional level (with appropriate review by each department).

How Many Statements of Intended Educational (Student) Outcomes Are Necessary for Each Program?

This question is similar to that asked by freshmen regarding their first composition, "How long must it be?" The answer is similar to that allegedly offered by faculty: "Long enough to cover the subject without exhausting the reader." As a guide, it is suggested that between three and five statements of intended educational outcomes be identified for each academic program in the department, though there is nothing magical about these numbers.

Why such a small number of statements? There are both conceptual and pragmatic reasons to limit the number of statements of intended educational outcomes per academic program. From a conceptual standpoint, it is important to recognize that such statements are intended as overarching concepts which should span several courses and are not individual course objectives taken from each syllabus. However, from a practical point of view, there are many other reasons to limit the number of statements of intended educational outcomes being considered at one time.

First among these pragmatic reasons to limit the number of statements of intended educational outcomes is the fact that for every intended educational outcome, there will need to be developed at least one means of assessment to determine its accomplishment. Hence, the identification of intended educational outcomes forms the framework around which the assessment plan must be constructed. If a large number of intended educational outcomes are identified, then a large and elaborate (expensive) assessment mechanism will be necessary.

Who will accomplish this large and elaborate assessment program? The answer is that additional staff (administrators) will need to be employed, thus diminishing the educational focus of the institution, or that the burden will be "dumped" on the already heavily loaded faculty as part of their "professional" responsibility. Either solution is equally wrong and can be avoided with serious discussion among the faculty regarding the "most important" intended educational outcomes at any given time (See further discussion of this subject on page 25).

Second, in most academic programs, there are only a handful (three to five) of intended educational outcomes which the department can emphasize at one time. Departments frequently try to claim that they pursue a number of ends simultaneously; however, when reviewed carefully, there are relatively few common abilities or attitudes which we attempt to instill in our students.

Third, even if otherwise feasible, the establishment of a large number of intended educational outcomes and their necessary assessment procedures would constitute a stack of paper sufficient to "choke the proverbial horse" and little use would be made of the results. Thus, the effort and funds would have been expended only to realize little benefit because of the massiveness of the effort and data generated.

If there ever existed a subject in which the "KISS" (Keep It Simple Stupid) principle applied, outcomes assessment in higher education is that subject. Limiting the number of statements of intended educational (student) outcomes is the first (and many would say most important) step in adhering to that principle. Far better to limit the number of such statements, conduct successful programs of assessment to determine if you are accomplishing these intentions, and use the assessment results to improve student learning, than to curse a large pile of paper which has been difficult to produce, expensive, and is virtually useless.

The Accomplishment of Most Statements of Intended Educational (Student) Outcomes Should Be Ascertainable

The controversy regarding whether the results of what we attempt to accomplish through students is "measurable" has been among the bitterest within and most damaging to higher education. The bitterness has resulted from strongly held positions regarding the nature of our profession and disciplines, and the lack of a clear or common understanding regarding the use of the term "measurable." If academe moves away from a definition of "measurable" which (a) is characterized by a microscope and six-decimal place accuracy, (b) is entirely quantified and precludes qualitative judgments, and (c) is perceived primarily as standardized cognitive examinations, then part of that bitterness will begin to subside. The closer we move to a definition of "measurable" that includes a general judgment of whether students know, think, and can do most of what we intend for them, the easier agreement among faculty becomes. While there are a limited number of intended educational (student) outcomes for which accomplishment will be very difficult to ascertain, this number is surely relatively small.

It is important to get this bitterness behind us because the controversy has upon occasion led faculty to proclaim that since some intended educational outcomes aren't "measurable" (six-digit definition), then all intended educational outcomes aren't "measurable," and that the public should "trust us" and continue to provide funding for our endeavors. Frankly, the public is not buying that position anymore and identifies it as a "cop out." In many states, the requirements for assessment procedures as a form of accountability and reductions in relative funding are clear expressions of public displeasure and loss of confidence in the higher education enterprise

Through agreement upon a number of intended educational (student) outcomes (by far most of which are "measurable"—broad definition) the conduct of appropriate assessment procedures to determine their accomplishment, and the sharing of these accomplishments with the public, a large degree of public confidence in higher education can be restored, and that will serve all types of institutions.

How High Should Intended Educational (Student) Outcomes Be Set?

One of the practical questions departmental administrators will face is posed above. The relatively straightforward answer is to be realistic considering the academic abilities of the students as they enter the program, the level of rigor expected in the classes, and the resources available to support the instructional process.

There is nothing to be gained by setting criteria for intended outcomes (average scores, percentile ranks, etc.) unreasonably high. If an institution operates a virtually open door admissions program, with the result that entering students have diagnostic test scores averaging in the 20–30 percentile range (compared with the national population), there is little chance that its graduates will average in the 80–90 percentile range on most standardized cognitive examinations. What purpose has been served by setting intended outcomes at that level? The department has looked foolish, the students have been driven beyond reason to attain an unrealistic expectation, and all concerned record a frustrating experience from what may have been a considerable accomplishment (graduation of students who clearly meet or exceed professional standards).

On the other hand, there is also little to be gained from setting intended educational outcomes at such a modest level that any "warm, breathing body" even indirectly exposed to the instructional program can meet them. The educational program at any institution should represent a reasonable challenge for both students and faculty.

It has been the authors' experience that most institutions at which "warm breathing body" statements of intended educational (student) outcomes were encountered have been institutions that failed to distinguish these assessment activities from the procedures that exist on all our campuses for evaluation of individual faculty and other employees. It is absolutely imperative that in word, as well as deed, the assessment processes initiated on the campus be held separate from necessary evaluative procedures concerning individuals. Unless this takes place, faculty, being human beings, will insure that they "look good" regarding intended educational outcomes in order to merit increases in rank, salary, or possibly tenure.

In setting criteria for intended educational outcomes, faculty are answering the "ought" question regarding their programming. Having answered the question "What should students be able to think, know, or do?", the "ought" question focuses upon how well should they be able to perform the intended educational or student outcomes identified. The institutions profiled in *Assessment Case Studies* reported almost uniformly that the tendency for the faculty to use assessment results to improve programming was directly linked to the extent to which they identified the criteria for program success (answering the "ought" question) before the actual assessment process took place. When reviewing actual assessment results, if a discrepancy exists between what faculty had previously stated students ought to be able to do (the ideal state) and the actual results reflecting what they can do, faculty will in most cases take the necessary corrective action. However, without such a criterion against which to reflect actual student performance, the tendency to use the data to improve the program is substantially diminished.

At what point in the process should the department establish these criteria for program success, as part of the intended educational (student) outcome or as part of the means of assessment? If in these early stages of identification of the statements of intended educational outcomes faculty become too involved in identification of the answer to the "ought" question and the specific means of assessment to be utilized for measurement, then the focus of the process shifts naturally from student expectations to measurement or assessment. While expression of criteria for program success is certainly possible in the statement of intended educational or student outcomes, "the majority of graduates will be employed upon graduation," in most cases, the identification of this criteria for program success is best selected in conjunction with identification in the means of assessment to be discussed in the next chapter, "50% or more of the students completing the Graduating Student Questionnaire will indicate that they are currently employed or have accepted a job offer at the close of their program."

Criteria for success are often set at both the *primary* (overall) and *secondary* (detailed) levels as reference points or benchmarks for program performance. *Primary* criteria for success establish overall targets for program performance such as "the average score of graduates on the ETS Major Field Test in Literature will be at or near the 50th percentile." The potential use of results for program improvement can be greatly enhanced by also setting more detailed criteria for success which require *secondary* analysis such as "and no subscale score will be below the 30th percentile." While overall program performance may meet or exceed primary criteria for success, faculty are informed through consideration of this secondary analysis of those more specific areas, scales, or individual items falling short of their expectations. Whenever feasible, faculty should set not only primary, but secondary criteria for success and conduct detailed analysis of assessment information to the level necessary for it to be of use.

Preparing Statements of Intended Educational (Student) Outcomes

Role of the Departmental Administrator

The position of the departmental administrator (head, chairperson, etc.) is among the most difficult in higher education and calls for actions ranging from those that can be described as "arbitrary and capricious" to the totally collegial model. In this particular instance, the departmental administrator can assume no more of a leadership role than "first among equals" due to the fact that the issues raised by setting intended educational (student) outcomes are clearly "curricular" in nature, as opposed to "administrative" decisions concerning course scheduling, salary increases, etc. In many ways the departmental administrator's role can be described as that of a "facilitator." Yet those to whom the departmental administrator reports will undoubtedly hold him/her responsible for implementation.

What actions by the departmental administrator are appropriate? Among the actions departmental administrators may undertake to further identification of intended educational outcomes without alienating their colleagues are the following:

- *Gathering information regarding what is expected*—Communication to the departmental faculty of the answers to those questions posed on page 15 is certainly among the duties that can be accomplished.

- *Motivating the faculty to take part*—The single factor reported as the greatest impediment to implementation of educational outcomes assessment is "faculty indifference or resistance." Faculty are frequently indifferent due to a measure of ingrained cynicism, already heavy instructional loads, and resistance based upon allegedly philosophical grounds. The departmental administrator should put the best face on the requirement by seeking to explain the intrinsic value to the departmental faculty of taking part in the activity. Further, integration of credit for participation in the outcomes assessment effort into the departmental and institutional reward structure for faculty will also aid in motivation (See Chapter III of *Assessment Case Studies* for further discussion).

- *Provision of coordination and logistical support*—Establishing the meetings, scheduling the times by which certain decisions should be reached, and providing typing and other services are clearly within the responsibility of the departmental administrator.

- *Getting things moving in a participative, nonconfrontational manner*—Some departmental administrators have found that a useful way to start the discussion regarding intended outcomes is to request that each member of the faculty forward a list of the five most important things which a graduate of each degree program should know or be able to do. From that submission, the departmental administrator can identify those areas in which there is common agreement and focus departmental discussions on refinement of these areas and selection of several others.

It is important that the departmental administrator not force his/her will on the group or appear to do so. Likewise, the statements of intended educational outcomes should not represent the product of several hours behind the departmental administrator's closed door. Unless the faculty feels actively involved in the process of identification of intended educational outcomes, they will not participate in identification of means of assessment, assist in the assessment procedures, or utilize the results of the assessment process.

Role of the Departmental Faculty
The responsibility for faculty control of the curriculum in an institution's degree programs is not challenged by the implementation of educational (student) outcomes assessment activities. Quite the contrary, faculty are requested (or required) to exercise their prerogatives regarding the curriculum, which only they can and should control, perhaps more so than in the past.

As pretentious as the words above may sound, there's some need for such bravado as departmental faculty are asked to address the issue of intended educational outcomes. Not only is the notion of outcomes or results-oriented thinking (as opposed to "process"—see earlier discussion) new and difficult, but discussions focusing on the program as a whole may also be among the first of their kind in the departments. It is not uncommon that strong differences of opinion (which may have been avoided in the past) based on differing points of view concerning the discipline are voiced. In some instances, there exists the danger that faculty will not readily step forward and assume their proper role in identification of intended educational outcomes. In such instances, there is the temptation to "do it for them" in order to meet the departmental deadline. This temptation must be resisted by the departmental administrator, and efforts to involve as many of the faculty as possible in meaningful ways should be redoubled.

Potential Problems in Preparation of Statements of Intended Educational (Student) Outcomes

Faculty Ownership
As just described, motivation of the faculty to take part in identification of intended educational outcomes is likely to be the primary difficulty encountered in implementation. While it is unlikely that all faculty will take part in any departmental endeavor, the offer to take part must be visibly extended on several occasions and the majority of the faculty must play an active role. Endorsement of the effort by the faculty governance structure, in addition to the motivational suggestions mentioned earlier, may help to stimulate participation. Regardless of the means utilized, the statements of intended educational (student) outcomes must be identified closely with the professional judgment of a majority of the faculty in the department.

Limiting the Number of Statements

Once the motivational issue is resolved, the next issue encountered will probably be arriving at a consensus among the departmental faculty regarding the most important three to five statements of intended educational outcomes. Since faculty frequently tend to function in relation to their courses (a portion of a program) and come to naturally believe in the importance of that material in their courses, it is understandable that many faculty will suggest compilation of their course objectives as intended educational outcomes for the academic program. This often results in 30 to 40 or more such statements being suggested among which three to five need to be selected. Review of the statements suggested should identify common themes (bodies of knowledge), abilities, and attitudes that can be discerned among those submitted for consideration. From this review, a number of statements can be drawn, though care will need to be taken not to generalize the description of intended educational outcomes (for the sake of being inclusive) to the point that they loose their identity or sufficient specificity for assessment purposes.

Understanding that consensus will never be completely achieved among the faculty, one means through which to maintain relative harmony among the departmental faculty is to explain the selection of the three to five statements of intended educational outcomes as the "short list" taken from the "long list" of all intended educational outcomes submitted (see Figure 3 on the following page). For practical reasons, the three to five statements selected for the short list are all that the institution and the department can initially afford to establish assessment procedures. Once assessment of these intended educational outcomes is accomplished, some of the statements from the short list may be returned to the long list and statements from the long list moved to the short list for the purpose of initiation of assessment activities. There is no circumstance under which intended educational outcomes for a program need go unchanged for an extended period.

The key to establishing a usable short list of intended educational outcomes is their selection from the long list. If the departmental faculty find that their statements of intended educational outcomes on the short list contain a series of commas, semicolons, or conjunctions, there is a considerable probability that a number of statements from the long list have been combined to establish one intended outcome on the short list. This can work very well where the different items on the longer list speak to the same theme, body of knowledge, or skill. However, in many (most) cases, appearance of these punctuation marks and conjunctions signifies no more than the departmental faculty's desire to be "politically correct" and not to exclude any person from the process. This is particularly the case in smaller departments or those composed of a significant number of untenured faculty members. However, the result of this action is chaos when separate means of assessment must be identified for each of the formerly separate intended educational outcomes specified. At that point, accomplishment of each of the formerly separate intended educational outcomes from the long list will need to be verified (moving the number of assessment activities per academic program from 6–10 to 18–30) and the burden of assessment will become so great as to bog down the process. The key to survival and success in the implementation process at the departmental level is keeping the process simple by faculty selecting the most important intended educational outcomes from the long list.

Figure 3

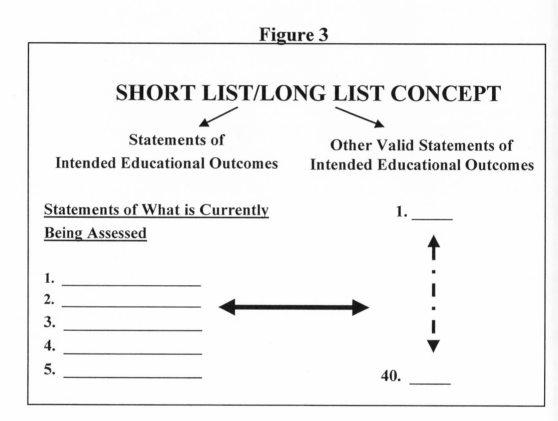

Backing into Intended Educational Outcomes from Assessment Means
Human beings imitate one another and educators are certainly no exception. A dangerous problem which may well be encountered is the faculty member who says "the department similar to ours at another college is using the XYZ examination for assessment and I think we should seriously consider its use." The acceptance of a means of assessment utilized by another institution or an available standardized examination indicates that the department has adopted at least the majority of the statements of intended educational outcomes upon which the other institution or test maker has based the means of assessment. While this may be the department's intention, countless departmental faculty have forfeited their prerogatives regarding control of the curriculum by taking this easy way out and unintentionally accepting another group's statements of intended educational outcomes as their own.

Revisions to Statements of Intended Educational (Student) Outcomes

One set of apparent problems, the need to revise statements of intended educational outcomes, will only become evident once means of assessment have been identified. The best statements of intended educational (student) outcomes indicating "appreciation," "understanding," etc., often fade in their attractiveness when faced with the need to identify a means through which to assess or ascertain accomplishment of such lofty ideas. It is quite normal that a number of statements of intended educational outcomes initially established will undergo refinement during identification of the means for assessment of their accomplishment. It is also possible that faced with a lack of ability to identify an appropriate means of assessment, some statements may be moved back to the long list and more assessable statements moved to the short list.

Examples of Statements of Intended Educational (Student) Outcomes

General Comments

On the following pages are four examples (Figures 4-7) of statements of intended educational outcomes, two for four-year institutions and two depicting such statements at two-year colleges. The following general comments relate to all four examples:

a. *Common Format*—While no accrediting agency or, to our knowledge, state agency requires a certain format (form) upon which to record statements of intended educational outcomes, many faculty and departmental administrators are more comfortable if they have a form to complete or common format. The format in which the examples have been presented is one means for expressing the necessary components on one page which clearly shows the relationships between the Expanded Statement of Institutional Purpose and Intended Educational Outcomes. During this publication these examples will be extended to the complete implementation model. However, as useful as this format is to depict the important relationships existing in this process, the feasibility of graphic expression of these components by many departments is not great. Therefore, the Assessment Record Book, described in the appendices to this publication, has been provided to ease departmental record keeping.

b. *Relationship to Expanded Statements of Institutional Purpose*—Each of these examples is linked to the appropriate example Expanded Statements of Institutional Purposes contained in Appendix A, B, or C of *A Practitioner's Handbook* (3rd ed). For institutions implementing educational (student) outcomes assessment at the departmental level within an institutional effectiveness context, this linkage to and support of the institution's purpose is absolutely essential. However, not

Figure 4

Undergraduate English Program
Two-Column Model

Expanded Statement of Institutional Purpose

Mission Statement:

The principal focus of Our University's curricular program is undergraduate education in the liberal arts and science...

▼

Goal Statement:

... all graduates of baccalaureate level will have developed a depth of understanding in their major field.

Program Intended Educational Outcomes:

1. Students completing the baccalaureate program in English will compare very favorably in their knowledge of literature with those students completing a similar program nationally.

2. Graduates will be able to critique a brief draft essay, pointing out the grammatical, spelling, and punctuation errors.

3. Students completing the baccalaureate program will be capable of writing an acceptable journal article.

Figure 5

Accounting Degree Program
Two-Column Model

Expanded Statement of Institutional Purpose

Mission Statement:

The principal focus of Our University's curricular program is undergraduate education in the liberal arts and sciences...

Goal Statement:

All graduates of baccalaureate programs will have developed a depth of understanding in their major field...

Program Intended Educational Outcomes:

1. Students completing the baccalaureate program in accounting will be well prepared for their first position in the field.

2. Baccalaureate graduates of the accounting program will find ready employment in the field.

3. Graduates will be experienced in the use of personal computers for accounting procedures.

Figure 6

Transfer Program
Two-Column Model

Expanded Statement of Institutional Purpose

Mission Statement:

… an open-admission, community-based, comprehensive college designed to provide inexpensive, quality educational opportunities (college transfer, career/technical and continuing education) …

Goal Statements:

Serve traditional students seeking the first two years of instruction leading to a bachelor's degree.
a. Recipients of …degree will be readily accepted …
b. Graduates will complete their bachelor's degrees at …same rate….as native students
c. Courses offered … as a foundation or prerequisite for courses at four-year colleges will be accepted for that purpose

Program Intended Educational Outcomes:

1. Students transferring will find courses taken fully accepted as prerequisites for junior and senior level courses at four-year colleges.

2. After one year of adjustment to the four-year college, the grades of students transferring will be similar to those of students who initially enrolled at four-year colleges

3. Graduates transferring to a four-year as full-time students will complete their baccalaureate degree at almost the same rate as those students originally enrolling at the four-year college.

Figure 7

Automotive Technology Program
Two-Column Model

Expanded Statement of Institutional Purpose

Mission Statement:

Your Community College is an open-admission, community-based, comprehensive college.

Goal Statement:

Serve persons of all ages in preparing for job entry and careers in a variety of fields.

Program Intended Educational Outcomes:

1. Graduates of the Automotive Technology Program will be successfully employed in the field.

2. Graduates of the Automotive Technology Program will be technically proficient.

3. Employers of the Automotive Technology Program graduates, in the five-county service area, will be pleased with the education received by their employees.

all departments should expect to support each goal statement within an institution's Expanded Statement of Institutional Purpose. Most academic departments will identify only one (perhaps two) goal statements specifically supported by their academic programs. Departments implementing educational outcomes assessment in other than an institutional effectiveness context may choose to disregard this component of the model.

c. *Simple Wording*—The statements of intended educational outcomes are uniformly simple and straightforward. They are non-technical expressions offered by the faculty in the department regarding what they believe students should know, be able to do, or think upon completion of their programs. In several instances, the general criteria for assessment have been identified within the statements of intended educational outcomes while in others even a general identification has been left for the next phase of the effort—identification of the means of assessment and criteria for success.

Concluding Comments Regarding Identification of Intended Educational (Student) Outcomes

Setting intended educational (student) outcomes for an academic program is a step often overlooked because:

- The department may not be required to identify them.
- Of the threat of "assessment" which dominates the scene.
- Identification of intended educational outcomes can cause disagreements among faculty.

However, on the positive side, setting intended educational (student) outcomes will:

- Establish a positive focus for the assessment effort and reduce its cost.
- Serve a number of constructive uses in curriculum reform outside of outcomes assessment.
- Provide a natural "market" or use for the information resulting from the assessment procedures described in the next chapter.

Once intended educational (student) outcomes are identified for each academic program, the justification for "assessment," and many of the questions surrounding it, will become much clearer and less threatening.

Chapter III

ASSESSMENT OF STUDENT LEARNING

A Means or an End?

Few terms elicit as much anxiety in academe as does the term "assessment." Within the various contexts described earlier, assessment of student learning is considered as both a means and an end. The legislative mandate that certain cognitive tests be administered and the results reported is an example of assessment as an end. This relatively punitive type of requirement serves little purpose and adds further to the negative connotations regarding assessment. On the other hand, when assessment is perceived as a means or bridge between intended educational (student) outcomes and use of the results of assessment to improve instructional programs and student learning, much of the implicit threat of the assessment process is removed. All accreditation-based assessment initiatives characterize assessment as a means for improvement of instructional programming. Within this publication the role of assessment as a means is emphasized.

Assessment Is "No Big Deal"

The greatest fear is that of the unknown, and "assessment" is no exception. Among the few guarantees regarding implementation of assessment procedures is that an inventory of current campus practices will reveal several areas (departments, programs, etc.) that already have functional assessment programs in place. These colleagues have been "doing assessment" for their own sake, have not been overwhelmed with the task, and appear to be otherwise relatively normal faculty without particular experience in evaluation methodology.

Assessment activities don't need a rocket scientist to be implemented. They do need careful review of the assessment options (means) available and consideration of the statements of intended educational (student) outcomes and resources available (usually small), as well as the specific requirements placed upon the department. The perfect means of assessment will never exist; however, choices will need to be made and implemented based upon the department's judgment of the best means available at the time. To further compensate for this lack of perfection in means of assessment, it is suggested the several or multiple means of assessment be identified for each intended outcome.

Means of Assessment Available to Instructional Departments

Qualitative and Quantitative Means of Assessment
Qualitative means of assessment describe those evaluations in which a holistic judgment concerning a subject is made. Among the best known examples of such qualitative assessment activities are Portfolio Reviews, Public Performances, Oral Examinations, or Dissertation Defenses. In each of these means, there is considerable flexibility on the part of the evaluator, and the assessment takes place within a given context. Such qualitative assessment has a rich tradition (particularly in the fine and performing arts) in higher education; however, it exhibits several limitations:

- *Identification of criteria for success*—Due to the relative subjectivity of most qualitative means of assessment, the identification of specific criteria for assessment and standards for success is difficult.
- *Objectivity of evaluators*—Because those conducting the evaluations are frequently the same faculty who have taught the students during their program, a serious question concerning the objectivity of the evaluators can be raised. This issue may be resolved by the use of external evaluators.
- *Consistency or reliability of judgment*—Assuming that the criteria for assessment can be identified, major problems exist in the consistency with which these necessarily judgmental factors are implemented by different evaluators or from year to year. A solution, though time consuming, is the thorough training of evaluators using identical procedures each year.

Even with the limitations outlined above, qualitative assessment is a legitimate form of assessment which should be seriously considered in any departmental decision regarding the choice of means of assessment.

Quantitative assessment, that form of evaluation characterized by its identification of individual components and provision of quantitative scores, is the form of assessment more commonly implemented. While there are innumerable ways to subdivide quantitative assessment, we have chosen the following three-part taxonomy for ease of discussion: Cognitive Means of Assessment, Assessment of Behavioral Change and Performance, and Attitudinal Assessment. More extensive resource sections regarding each of these subjects are contained in Chapter III of *A Practitioner's Handbook* (3rd ed.) to supplement the following brief discussion of each type of assessment.

Cognitive Means of Assessment
While there are some splendid theoretical arguments concerning the precise meaning of "cognition" in clinical and experimental jargon, the term is used in assessment circles in relationship to what most faculty would identify as learning or knowledge. This concept of knowledge is differentiated from the students' ability to use knowledge (behavior/performance) and their feeling toward the subject or field (attitudes). Cognitive assessment frequently takes place at the beginning of higher education (placement, diagnostic, or entrance examinations), after completion of the general education compo-

nent of students' degree programs (rising junior test), and at the conclusion of their course of study (degree program). While some departments, due to their service course orientation, will be concerned about the cognitive assessment of general education, most departmental attention will be focused on cognitive assessment at the close of a student's degree program.

Regretfully, most faculty when thinking of assessment immediately see a student taking a standardized cognitive examination. That is unfortunate, since knowledge is certainly only one component of our intended educational (student) outcomes, and standardized cognitive examinations represent only one type of cognitive assessment. Nonetheless, such instruments are a highly visible form of cognitive assessment.

There are three general types of cognitive standardized examinations commonly utilized in higher education at the end of the students' baccalaureate degree program: professional/graduate school admissions tests, licensure examinations, and standardized achievement tests specifically designed for assessment purposes.

The advantages to utilization of such standardized cognitive examinations include that they are (Ewell, 1987):

- Relatively easy to administer.
- Acceptable in terms of faculty and staff time invested.
- Generally less open to charges of subjectivity or bias by the public (or their representatives).
- Nationally normed for comparisons across institutions.
- Statistically valid and reliable.

However, these instruments exhibit serious disadvantages, including that they may (Ewell, 1987):

- Not reflect the department's intended educational (student) outcomes.
- Frequently provide only aggregate scores often not meaningful to assessment of specific intended educational (student) outcomes.
- Compare institutional data to an inappropriate national normative group.
- Be relatively expensive to purchase and score.

As related earlier, the most serious limitation of such standardized cognitive examinations is their potential lack of relation to intended educational (student) outcomes of the program. The first question which must be considered in evaluation of any assessment means is "Does it measure accomplishment of what we intended?" The often negative answer to this question regarding standardized cognitive tests, as well as growing confidence in the institution's own ability to construct comprehensive examinations, are part of the reason that reliance on standardized cognitive measures has declined in recent years (El-Khawas, 1993). Just as the quality and potential usefulness of such instruments has improved, roughly seven out of ten times when faculty review standardized instruments in their field, they are rejected.

Early in the assessment movement, the primary means of standardized cognitive assessment was the achievement portion (subject test) of the Graduate Record Examination (GRE). While this was virtually the only national available standardized cognitive examination at the baccalaureate level, the GRE had been developed for a purpose (screening students for entry to graduate school) unrelated to assessment. While extensive use of these GRE achievement tests as an end of program cognitive assessment was made, its inadequacies for this purpose became quickly apparent.

Several years ago, the Educational Testing Service (ETS) which is the producer of the GRE series began marketing their Major Field Achievement Test (MFAT) developed from a similar knowledge base as the GRE, but for assessment purposes. MFAT examinations are available primarily in the same fields as those developed for the GRE as shown below:

Biology	Mathematics
Chemistry	Music
Computer Science	Physics
Economics	Political Science
Education	Psychology
History	Sociology
Literature in English	

These MFAT examinations have proven to be a considerable improvement for assessment purposes over the GRE due to: (a) the availability of specimen copies to compare with departmental intended educational outcomes, (b) score reports in more useful subscales, and (c) more appropriate normative groups. In the summer of 1990, ETS introduced it's first MFAT (Business Administration) developed independently from the GRE. MFAT is a reasonable place to start a department's review of standardized cognitive assessment means should one be available in the field. At the very least, departmental faculty will have the opportunity to review what a national panel of faculty in their discipline has identified as the primary body of knowledge in the field.

The Area Concentration Achievement Test (ACAT) produced at Austin Peay State University in Tennessee represents another viable source of standardized testing in the major at the end of baccalaureate programs. The ACAT examinations are available in the following fields: agriculture, art, biology, criminal justice, geology, history, literature, political science, psychology and social work. They feature a standardized item bank in each field from which institutions are free to select only those scales which "fit" the individual institution's curriculum. This process, to a large extent, customizes these standardized examinations to an institution's individual curriculum. The smaller number of institutions utilizing ACAT constitutes a limitation which potential purchasers should consider.

In the past, the very limited number of nationally standardized tests available for occupational/technical programs in the two-year college was a significant limitation to assessment of these programs. However, during the last several years the development of the Job Ready Tests (formerly marketed as the Student Occupational Competency Achievement Test) by the National Occupational Competency

Testing Institute (NOCTI) and the Engineering Technician and Technologist Certification Programs conducted by the National Institute for Certification in Engineering Technologies (NICET) has contributed substantially to filling this void. The Job Ready Tests cover a wide variety of fields, from child care through horticulture to electronics, and consist of both a written objective test and performance test that are institutionally administered. The NICET certification examinations are available in a much narrower set of fields directly related to the engineering technologies. These NICET examinations also consist of written cognitive examination as well as practical performance tests but are only administered at state testing locations several times each year.

In addition to the MFAT, four-year college departmental faculty should consider both professional school admissions tests and licensure examinations as a means of standardized cognitive assessment, if for no other reason than the fact that many of their students already take such examinations. Professional schools admissions test are an apparent source of assessment data; however, they suffer from two specific limitations. While parts of some such examinations such as the Medical School Admissions Test do measure knowledge, others such as the Graduate Management Aptitude Test (GMAT), the Law School Admission Test (LSAT), and the Dental Aptitude Test (DAT) measure aptitude or general intelligence far more than achievement. Second, because these test are designed for screening purposes, they are highly secure instruments which the faculty will not have an opportunity to review in detail and will receive only highly aggregated results.

Licensure examinations taken by students prior to entry into a profession (Bar, Medical, Nursing, Teaching, Certified Public Accountant, etc.) represent a potentially very useful type of cognitive assessment in the major. Most such licensure examinations vary somewhat by state in either content and/or the amount of institutional feedback of results available. Ideally, their content should relate closely with the intended educational outcomes of the degree programs preparing students for these professions. Where available, the results of such licensure constitute "instant assessment data" for those institutions implementing under the pressure of time.

While the standardized cognitive means of assessment outlined have improved substantially in recent years (as indicated earlier), the clear trend among institutions is toward a more locally developed end of program cognitive measures (El-Khawas, 1993). Among the advantages of construction of locally developed cognitive examinations are the following (Ewell, 1987):

a. *Reflection of the specific intended educational (student) outcomes identified by the department*—Because of its local development, the examination can be designed to exactly match the intended educational outcomes of the department.

b. *Ability to conduct detailed analysis*—Since the results are available in their entirety, they can be carefully analyzed to determine areas of the curriculum which are supporting accomplishment of intended educational outcomes and those which are not.

c. *Flexibility in format*—Because the examination will be locally scored, a combination of essay, multiple choice, and other type items may be utilized.

d. *Faculty ownership*—Based upon their heavy involvement in all aspects of preparation and grading, departmental faculty have no question regarding the legitimacy of the examination or their ownership and tend to use the results of such examinations more readily.

Despite the impressive advantages cited above, there are numerous disadvantages to the construction and utilization of locally developed cognitive means of assessment. Among these are (Ewell, 1987):

a. *Lack of external credibility*—If the department is implementing in response to a state accountability mandate, there is little likelihood that locally developed instruments will be acceptable. Within accreditation related contexts for implementation, locally developed instruments are acceptable.

b. *Lack of comparative data*—The inability to compare student achievements with other institutions limits the nature of statements of intended educational outcomes.

c. *High faculty effort to develop, administer and maintain*—The greatest disadvantage of this approach is the exceedingly great amount of effort needed to develop and maintain such locally developed instruments over a long period of time. While relatively short bursts of faculty energy may be harnessed to develop such tests, most departmental faculty are simply unwilling (in the face of their other duties) to commit high levels of effort to this process over an extended period.

The experience of the case studies institutions in the matter of locally developed comprehensive examinations was disappointing. Fewer such examinations than expected were reported as being implemented by faculty and departments at these eleven institutions. The primary reason most often cited for failure to develop such tests was the lack of release time for development of such instruments. This lack of release time is in agreement with such policies that exist at most institutions nationally and is obviously a primary impediment to the use of locally developed comprehensive examinations. It is the authors' opinion that given the amount of work inherent therein, the effort bearing directly upon development of comprehensive locally developed assessment means should be recognized in some way. This recognition may take the form of summer employment, institutionally identified release time, or informal reduction of a faculty member's teaching load by the department chair during the time the test is being prepared. Once the comprehensive locally developed examination is prepared, then, in the authors' opinion, administration, grading, and maintenance should be accomplished as part of a normal faculty load without extra recognition or compensation.

While cognitive assessment is clearly only one form of ascertaining accomplishment of intended student outcomes, it is without much question the dominant form. Students attend our institutions primarily to learn or acquire knowledge. Cognitive assessment validates their accomplishment of that purpose. For a more technical discussion of specific standardized cognitive examinations and the sources from which they can be obtained, see the Resource Section, "Cognitive Assessment Instruments: Availability and Utilization" by Krotseng and Pike in the 3rd edition of *A Practitioner's Handbook.*

Assessment of Behavioral Change and Performance

Just as cognitive assessment is the most commonly identified form of assessment, assessment of changes in student behavior and performance is probably the most overlooked form of assessment. This form of assessment relates to what a student *does* or *can do* as a result of accomplishing previously identified statements of intended educational (student) outcomes and is composed of the slightly differing concepts of behavior and performance.

In behavioral assessment one observes what a student does following a given treatment (completion of a degree program) and compares that behavior with the intended educational (student) outcomes of the program. This observation is made concerning an event in the student's life which is not regulated, contrived, or designed for the purposes of assessment.

Examples of such diverse behavioral assessment activities include: employment, admission to graduate school, church attendance, and voting. Many of our degree programs are primarily oriented toward preparation of individuals for employment. Thus the primary criteria for success of the program becomes "Did the graduate find employment in the field?", a matter ascertained by observing the behavior (getting a job) of the graduate upon completion of the program. Likewise, many programs are focused principally on preparation of students for graduate work. The success of such programs may be primarily gauged by the acceptance of baccalaureate graduates into graduate school. The primary purpose of the transfer program of two-year colleges is to prepare students for successful transfer to a four-year college. Without observation of graduate performance at four-year colleges, the two-year college transfer program's success is difficult to ascertain or gauge.

Activities reported by alumni some time after graduation, reflecting attitudes or values that were intended educational (student) outcomes of their program are among the most powerful forms of behavioral assessment. To the Bible college whose students are required to enroll in 30 or more hours of courses related to religion, there is little more gratifying or relevant than responses to an alumni survey indicating a regular pattern of church attendance and leadership by its former students. To the English department faculty who have identified "development of a lifelong love of reading" as an intended educational outcome of their program in Literature, what more satisfying result than alumni who report owning small libraries in their homes, reading several works of fiction each month, or teaching others to read. While observation or reporting of events in the lives of students or graduates is not easily accomplished, it can provide some of the best assessment results received by faculty.

Performance type assessment is similar to behavioral assessment in that it seeks to observe what the student does; however, in this instance, the student is asked to "perform" as a matter of assessment. Few consumers are concerned with the amount of theory that graduates of an associate degree program in Automotive Technology have acquired. They want to know "Can they fix my car?"; hence, such programs tend to identify relatively pragmatic statements of intended educational outcomes, and performance type assessment mechanisms such as that described in the example on page 49. Likewise, while knowledge of medicine is an important requisite for surgeons, it is their ability to perform successful surgery that is assessed during their internship/residency.

The advantages of behavioral or performance assessment relate to:

* Their ability to provide evidence directly bearing on some of the most important intended educational outcomes.
* In the case of behavior, the lack of intrusiveness or very limited amount of additional effort on the part of the graduate to provide the information needed, and the ability to extend such assessment activities to ascertain accomplishment of longer term intended educational outcomes.
* In the case of performance, the opportunity to control external variables to place the students in exactly the surroundings in which the intended educational outcomes should be demonstrated in their professional lives.

The principal disadvantages of behavioral and performance related assessment are:

* Limited applicability of the approach to some academic disciplines.
* Need to receive necessary information from alumni and other institutions (transfer institutions for two-year college students and graduate level institutions for four-year college students).
* Cost of preparation and maintenance of performance tests (particularly over an extended period of time).
* Considerable amount of time necessary to train assessors of student performance to insure reliability.

Due to their nature, few standardized performance means of assessment are available, leaving most to be developed locally. Likewise, much behavioral observation information is gained from local sources or developed instruments.

One type of performance assessment that overlaps with qualitative means and appears at the outset to be particularly attractive (some might even say seductive) is portfolio assessment. In portfolio assessment the performance of students is reviewed based upon a longitudinal collection of their work made during their matriculation at the institution. In the authors' opinion, while this is a valid means of assessment, in some aspects of the institution (particularly fine and performing arts and potentially English), it is more often abused than utilized correctly. Its abuse stems from the fact that faculty often see the collection of student class materials as a "quick and dirty" way to begin the assessment process and only when challenged with analysis of the portfolios, does the difficulty of the procedure become evident. Should the faculty desire to utilize portfolio assessment, it is recommended that the specific items from each class to be included in the portfolio be identified beforehand as well as the "quality" that should be demonstrated in each of these items in the portfolio. For additional information on performance assessment, see the resource section "Assessment of Behavioral Change and Performance" by Kinnick and Walleri in *A Practi-tioner's Handbook* (3rd ed.).

Attitudinal Assessment

It is impossible for faculty to provide all the knowledge and skills which students will need during their lifetime; however, the development of attitudes toward the discipline and the department's relative effectiveness in preparation of its graduates for life beyond the institution will undoubtedly occur. Thus, one form of intended educational outcome frequently identified by departmental faculty relates to the attitudes of students, graduates, alumni, and employers.

The identification of attitudes of students as they enter institutions and subsequently degree programs is frequently accomplished to determine their opinions regarding social, ethical, and moral issues. Such surveys may be utilized as benchmarks with which to compare similar responses after the students completion of the institution's general education or degree programs.

Determination of the students' attitudes concerning their discipline, course of study, or the educational support services provided by the institution is often sought at the point at which students leave the institution. This inquiry takes the form of a "graduating student" or "exiting student" (dropout) survey. This survey can be conducted either by written questionnaire or structured interview. The interview approach provides considerable flexibility to pursue particularly strong feelings on the part of individual students. The interviewers utilized by the institution should be carefully trained, nonthreatening, and unbiased.

Alumni surveys are among the most common forms of attitudinal assessment. They provide insight into the long-term development of students and valuable feedback concerning their behavior (employment, further schooling, etc.) after they leave the institution. Such data are frequently handicapped by the difficulty in identifying current attitudes of an unbiased sample of alumni and the fact that the responses of alumni may be to events, programs, and procedures long changed at the institution.

Frequently forgotten in discussions of attitudinal surveys is the determination of employer attitudes toward graduates. While there is a wide divergence of opinion between faculty, administrators, members of governing boards, and the public regarding what constitutes the characteristics of a quality institution, all such constituencies agree that the opinion of employers regarding the ability of institutional graduates is among the most important means through which to identify such an institution.

Attitudinal questionnaires designed for entering students, graduating students, alumni, etc. can be obtained from commercial sources or developed locally. American College Testing, Educational Testing Service, the College Board, and others provide relatively similar products that have been carefully developed, provide normative data with which to compare responses, and offer opportunities for the addition of locally developed items. Unfortunately, these instruments are relatively expensive per unit and offer little institutional identity. Locally developed attitudinal questionnaires can be customized to exactly match statements of intended educational outcomes (and administrative objectives in nonacademic departments), and exhibit a high level of institutional identification (colors, signatures, symbols, etc.) at a relatively low per-unit cost. However, locally developed instruments lack comparability of data and take a considerable amount of time and money to develop. Both commercial and locally developed questionnaires may be utilized to measure change in attitudes as well as attitudes at the end of programs.

Who should develop, support, and implement attitudinal assessment? The answer is clearly not the individual academic or administrative departments. If individual academic and administrative departments prepare their own attitudinal questionnaires:

- The considerable cost (time) needed for local development will be multiplied many fold.
- Students will be bombarded by questionnaires from their academic department, the library, the registrar, etc., and the response rate to all questionnaires will plummet.
- High-priced faculty will become heavily engaged in paper shuffling.
- Computer support will probably not be available for the multiple different formats for questionnaires surely to result.

While individual academic departments should have considerable input into the selection and/or the design of questionnaires to be utilized, and the opportunity to offer items specifically related to their degree program, they should not become involved with the logistics of distribution, processing, and analysis of attitudinal questionnaires. Their role is as one of the primary consumers of the information generated by attitudinal assessment. The central administration at the institution should provide survey research support. Through this mechanism, better surveys at a lower cost per unit are available throughout the institution.

The primary advantage of attitudinal assessment is that it can reflect the feelings and emotions of respondents as no other form of assessment is capable. The primary disadvantages are its considerable cost and the danger that respondents will provide only expected or socially acceptable answers.

While attitudinal assessment continues to be a popular form for evaluation of the accomplishment of intended educational outcomes, a number of regional accrediting associations are now less impressed with this means of assessment than initially was the case. One of the regional accrediting associations describes attitudinal assessment as an "indirect measure" of student achievement. Others are becoming more insistent that in addition to attitudinal assessment, programs should be able to demonstrate "direct measures" of student achievement. While attitudinal assessment remains a viable form of assessment, it clearly should no longer be depended upon as the *sole* means of assessment for any intended educational outcome.

Additional information concerning specific standardized attitudinal surveys and guidance for institutional level development of local instruments is continued in the Resource Section "Attitudinal Surveys in Institutional Effectiveness" by Raines, Bridger, and Wolff in *A Practitioner's Handbook* (3rd ed.).

The Nature of the Assessment Process

Who/What Is Being Assessed?

Among the most frequent misunderstandings regarding assessment is its focus or intent. Because on many occasions we must rely upon information originating from students or graduates, it is easy to assume that individual students or graduates are the focus of the assessment effort. In reality, aggregated accomplishments by students of intended educational outcomes is the primary available reflection of our programs and their results, which are the focus of the assessment effort.

What are the implications of understanding this critical difference in perspective?

- Not all students or graduates need take or respond to all means of assessment since a representative sample is sufficient for evaluation of the program.
- Criteria for intended educational (student) outcomes can be stated in terms of a portion of program graduates (as opposed to all) meeting an ambitious criteria.
- Assessment results reflect the accomplishments of the departmental faculty as a whole.

Having stated that the focus of assessment within the context described previously is the department's programs, it must also be indicated that departments may decide to share that focus with their students by requiring before graduation that students take a cognitive comprehensive examinations and achieve a minimum score, or pass a performance test. However, few departments have demonstrated sufficient confidence in their programmatic means of assessment to set other than minimal required levels of achievement by students prior to graduation from the institution. Sharing of the assessment focus with individual students by requiring a minimal score prior to issuance of a degree is practiced by very few institutions and is not recommended by these authors.

How Will Assessment Results Be Utilized?

The use of assessment results will certainly vary depending upon the context for implementation identified. If assessment is being implemented as an accountability mechanism in response to a state mandate, the primary use will be external to the institution to satisfy requirements and build public confidence; however, use within the department should also be encouraged. In any of the other context for assessment (institutional effectiveness, assessment of student achievement, or intrinsic motivation), the major use of assessment results will be internal to the institution for program improvement. Additionally, assessment results within the context of institutional effectiveness are utilized also (through intended educational outcomes linked to the institutional level) to validate the accomplishment of the institution's Expanded Statement of Institutional Purpose.

Use of assessment results in relation to individual faculty and students presents both pitfalls and opportunities. Because the focus of the assessment effort is on programs, it is both inappropriate and difficult to attempt to fix responsibility (particularly for shortcomings) on an individual faculty member. If the departmental faculty suspect that assessment is being conducted for personnel evaluation purposes, resistance will grow rapidly, vital participation in identifying intended educational outcomes will substantially diminish, any criteria set for assessment results will be extremely modest, results of assessment activities will be either challenged or unused, and the process will be perceived as a punitive administrative exercise. There is little that can "poison the well" more quickly than a few drops of evidence to support the latent paranoia regarding assessment that one finds on many campuses. To preclude potential misuse or misunderstandings regarding the use of assessment data, some campuses have found it particularly useful to establish a policy statement excluding the use of assessment results for personnel evaluation and approved by the Chief Executive Officer before implementation begins.

Use of assessment results regarding individual students has substantive implications for their motivation. If students are required to accomplish certain levels of achievement prior to being granted a degree (an unusual occurrence), student motivation is assured. On the other hand, if students are required only to "take" or "respond" to assessment measures without a minimum score requirement, or are asked to voluntarily take part in assessment activities, motivational problems will be quickly evidenced. Students must be convinced to take assessment seriously. Among the things that departmental faculty can do to encourage a sincere effort by students are the following:

- Imbed the means of assessment in classes using it once for grading purposes and a second time by the overall departmental faculty for assessment.
- Have faculty members acting as student advisors directly express the extent to which assessment, and the student's role in it, is taken seriously by the department.
- Indicate that assessment results will be among the first items reviewed when providing references to graduate school and for jobs.
- Appeal to the student's sense of interest in the discipline and the welfare of students who will follow them (a near last resort).

Through one means or another, sincere participation by students in assessment activities must be assured. The use of assessment results can be a powerful positive or negative motivator among students and faculty. The case study institutions found imbedding means of assessment in Capstone or other classes near the end of the program to be the most effective means of student motivation (see Chapter IV, *Assessment Case Studies*).

What Role Do Class Grades Play in Assessment?
In most instances, assessment requirements call for assessment beyond the course level. This requirement emphasizes (a) integration of the students' learning experiences across courses in their degree programs rather than from one course and (b) freeing the single faculty member (but not the combined departmental faculty) of the complete responsibility for assessment of program accomplishment through awarding of a grade. Like it or not, public

confidence in collegiate grading practices in individual courses is not exceptionally high. Employers have hired too many graduates who, though receiving passing marks and a degree from an institution, do not measure up to expectations.

There are two occasions in which course grades are acceptable as means of assessment. The first of these occasions is utilization of course grades in mainstream courses as a measure of the success of developmental or remedial education. In this case, students have moved from pre-college to college and crossed over into the next level of education. Likewise, grades or grade point averages of students transferring from two- to four-year institutions may be utilized as a means of assessment for the success of the transfer program at the two-year institution. As in the case of developmental education, these students also have moved to the next level of education beyond that which is being assessed.

The inability to utilize grades as a means of assessment is often questioned by faculty. One means to soften this injunction is through explanation of the Column and Row matrix shown in Figure 8. As faculty members, we have in mind certain criteria upon which we base grades and that we expect students to meet in their matriculation through our program and classes. These criteria are identified in the example as the rows Spelling, Grammar, Punctuation, and Structure shown in Figure 8. As faculty, we're used to the idea of looking down the column in this matrix

Figure 8

Relationship Between Individual Student Grading and Educational Outcomes Assessment

Individual Students Graded by Various Faculty					Criteria/Intended Educational Outcomes Average
Criteria Student1	**Student 2**	Student 3	Student 4	Student 5	
Spelling 3	**4 4**	1	2	3	**2.6**
Grammar 2	**5**	3	2	5	**3.4**
Punctuation 4	**5**	2	3	4	**3.6**
Structure 4	**3**	4	5	3	**3.8**
TOTAL 13	**17**	10	12	15	
Individual Student Grade C	**A**	D	C	B	

Total "Down the Columns" for Individual Student Grading
__Analyze "Across the Rows" for Assessment of Intended Educational Outcomes Accomplishment__

and awarding the student a grade at the foot of the column as signified by A, B, C, etc. The different columns in the matrix identify individual students whose collective results in each row of the matrix represent how well students overall passing through the curriculum did in relationship to the different criteria that we as faculty have already established. Thus the data for assessment purposes should be analyzed across the rows in the matrix to determine the extent to which the students are meeting the criteria otherwise known as intended educational (student) outcomes that have been established. In many cases, groups of faculty need only state their existing criteria in terms of intended educational (student) outcomes and reanalyze already existing data across the rows of the matrix (rather than down the columns for individual student grading purposes) in order to have readily usable assessment data available regarding their curriculum in a short time.

Importance of Multiple Measures

Descriptions of the assessment craft as imperfect or being in its infancy remain among the greatest understatements made. Not only are such statements correct, but the appropriateness of many instruments remains to be demonstrated in each institutional context. Not only is the MFAT in English Literature a relatively new instrument, but its suitability for assessment of the intended educational (student) outcomes identified by the English department at a given institution has yet to be demonstrated.

To compensate for the relative immaturity of many of the means of assessment available, several means of assessment should be identified for each intended educational (student) outcome.

By so doing, the results from each means may be compared as a measure of reliability of judgment and a backup will exist should one means prove totally unsatisfactory in practice.

Roles of the Faculty and Administration in Assessment

While the faculty have an important role to play in assessment, it is not as dominant as in identification of intended educational (student) outcomes. Among the appropriate faculty roles are:

- Participation in selection of the best means of assessment available to evaluate the accomplishment of their intended educational outcomes.
- Development, administration, grading, reporting of results, and maintenance of locally developed cognitive end of program examinations.
- Use of results to improve academic programs.

All of these roles describe departmental faculty who are interested in the selection of the appropriate means of assessment; may be responsible for design, administration, and evaluation of locally developed cognitive instruments; are among the primary consumers of information resulting from assessment activities; but who are not responsible for seeing that assessment takes place institution wide.

The primary responsibility for seeing that assessment activities take place should reside with the institution's administration in conjunction with an institutionally based faculty assessment committee in an oversight role. This administrative responsibility for seeing that assessment takes place is premised upon: (a) the need for a limited amount of additional funding for assessment initiatives, (b) the fact that many assessment activities can be more efficiently and effectively conducted at the institutional level, and (c) the already overburdened nature of most departmental faculty. Among the roles which departmental faculty should expect to see being played by central administration are the following:

- *Coordination of assessment activities under the oversight of a faculty committee*—The coordination, avoidance of duplication of effort, and design (if necessary) of common formats for expression of intended educational (student) outcomes and assessment results should flow from the central administration.

- *Provision of technical guidance*—Most academic departments cannot be expected to have technical expertise regarding test construction or survey research. Nor should individual departmental faculties be expected to stay abreast of the development of standardized means of assessment.

- *Logistical support*—The distribution and processing of questionnaires, administration of standardized examinations, and many other assessment measures are primarily clerical in nature. Given the already substantial loads carried by departmental faculty and the nature of the work, the provision of centralized logistical support makes both common and campus political sense.

There is a fine line between coordination/support of and control of any process; however, that is precisely the line that must not be crossed by the central administration. Responsibility for the substantive or policy aspects of the assessment process should be shared by departmental faculty, central administration, and an institutional level faculty oversight committee. The central administration's role should be perceived as coordination and support of activities commonly agreed upon.

Examples of the Use of Various Means of Assessment

Figures 9-12 on the following pages extend the English, Accounting, Auto Technology, and Transfer Examples provided earlier to the three-column models provided earlier in Figures 4-7 (pages 28-29) by identifying specific means of assessment and criteria for program success of each of the intended educational outcomes.

Several things should be pointed out concerning the following examples:

- Note the linkage from the Expanded Statement of Institutional Purpose through Goals, Intended Educational Outcomes, to Means of Assessment and Criteria. The linkage between these components enables the institution to trace the accomplishment of its stated purpose.

- In all four examples, the criteria for program success (average, percentage, etc.) have been identified in conjunction with the means of assessment. Where

Figure 9

Undergraduate English Program
Three-Column Model

Expanded Statement of Institutional Purpose	Program Intended Educational Outcomes:	Means of Program Assessment and Criteria for Success:
Mission Statement: The principal focus of Our University's curricular program is undergraduate education in the liberal arts and science... **Goal Statement:** ... all graduates of baccalaureate level will have developed a depth of understanding in their major field.	1. Students completing the baccalaureate program in English will compare very favorably in their knowledge of literature with those students completing a similar program nationally. 2. Graduates will be able to critique a brief draft essay, pointing out the grammatical, spelling, and punctuation errors. 3. Students completing the baccalaureate program will be capable of writing an acceptable journal article.	1a. The average score of the graduates of the BA program in English on the MFAT "Literature in English" will be at or near the 50th percentile compared to national results and no subscale score will be below the 30th percentile. 1b. On the graduating questionnaire, 90% of the English BA program graduates will "agree" or "strongly agree" with the statement "In the field of literature, I feel as well prepared as the majority of individuals nation wide who have completed a similar degree during the past year." 2a. As part of a "capstone course" during the final semester students will critique a short draft essay; identifying grammatical, spelling and punctuation errors. 80% of the program's graduates will identify 90% of the errors in the draft essay. Additionally, none of the 14 ruberics utilized to evaluate the student's critique will appear to be consistently unmet. 3a. A jury of English dept. faculty from an institution comparable to Our University will judge 80% of those journal articles submitted acceptable for publication. 3b. 20% of journal articles submitted will be published in student or other publications.

Figure 10

Accounting Degree Program
Three-Column Model

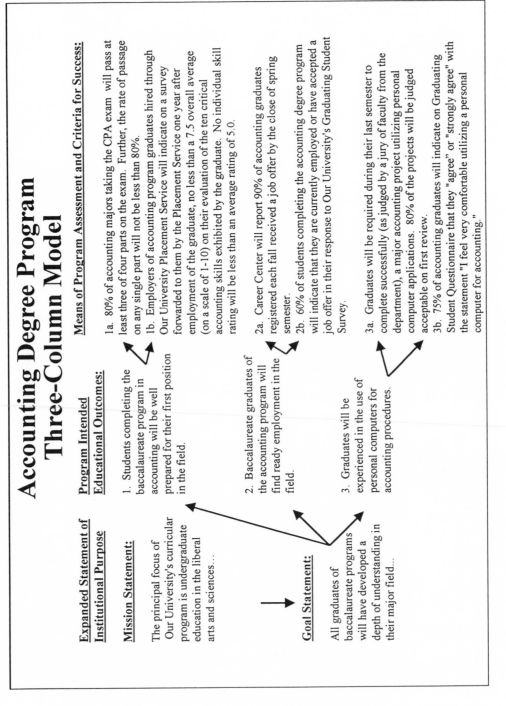

Expanded Statement of Institutional Purpose

Mission Statement:

The principal focus of Our University's curricular program is undergraduate education in the liberal arts and sciences...

Goal Statement:

All graduates of baccalaureate programs will have developed a depth of understanding in their major field...

Program Intended Educational Outcomes:

1. Students completing the baccalaureate program in accounting will be well prepared for their first position in the field.

2. Baccalaureate graduates of the accounting program will find ready employment in the field.

3. Graduates will be experienced in the use of personal computers for accounting procedures.

Means of Program Assessment and Criteria for Success:

1a. 80% of accounting majors taking the CPA exam will pass at least three of four parts on the exam. Further, the rate of passage on any single part will not be less than 80%.

1b. Employers of accounting program graduates hired through Our University Placement Service will indicate on a survey forwarded to them by the Placement Service one year after employment of the graduate, no less than a 7.5 overall average (on a scale of 1-10) on their evaluation of the ten critical accounting skills exhibited by the graduate. No individual skill rating will be less than an average rating of 5.0.

2a. Career Center will report 90% of accounting graduates registered each fall received a job offer by the close of spring semester.

2b. 60% of students completing the accounting degree program will indicate that they are currently employed or have accepted a job offer in their response to Our University's Graduating Student Survey.

3a. Graduates will be required during their last semester to complete successfully (as judged by a jury of faculty from the department), a major accounting project utilizing personal computer applications. 80% of the projects will be judged acceptable on first review.

3b. 75% of accounting graduates will indicate on Graduating Student Questionnaire that they "agree" or "strongly agree" with the statement "I feel very comfortable utilizing a personal computer for accounting."

Figure 11

Transfer Program
Three-Column Model

Expanded Statement of Institutional Purpose

Mission Statement:

… an open-admission, community-based, comprehensive college designed to provide inexpensive, quality educational opportunities (college transfer, career/technical and continuing education) …

Goal Statements:

Serve traditional students seeking the first two years of instruction leading to a bachelor's degree.

a. Recipients of …degree will be readily accepted …

b. Graduates will complete their bachelor's degrees at …same rate.…as native students

c. Courses offered … as a foundation or prerequisite for courses at four-year colleges will be accepted for that purpose

Program Intended Educational Outcomes:

1. Students transferring will find courses taken fully accepted as prerequisites for junior and senior level courses at four-year colleges.

2. After one year of adjustment to the four-year college, the grades of students transferring will be similar to those of students who initially enrolled at four-year colleges

3. Graduates transferring to a four-year as a full-time student will complete their baccalaureate degree at almost the same rate as those students originally enrolling at the four-year college.

Means of Program Assessment and Criteria for Success:

1. Each year one of the college's six academic departments will contact their counterparts at the three four-year institutions to whom most students transfer and all of courses designed to support the transfer of students will be found to be fully accepted as prerequisites by the faculty at the four-year institutions contacted.

2a. Analysis of four-year college data concerning the grades of transfer students will indicate that the differences between the average of transfer student's "GPA"s and that of native students is statistically insignificant one year after enrollment at the four-year college.

2b. Comparison of graduates' grades in typical classes at four-year colleges will result in no significant differences.

3a. Analysis of data received from three primary transfer student destinations will indicate that the difference in the average number of semesters to baccalaureate degree completion of full-time transfer students and students originally enrolling in four-year college is statistically insignificant.

Figure 12

Automotive Technology Program
Three-Column Model

Expanded Statement of Institutional Purpose

Mission Statement:

Your Community College is an open-admission, community-based, comprehensive college.

Goal Statement:

Serve persons of all ages in preparing for job entry and careers in a variety of fields.

Program Intended Educational Outcomes:

1. Graduates of the Automotive Technology Program will be successfully employed in the field.

2. Graduates of the Automotive Technology Program will be technically proficient.

3. Employers of the Automotive Technology Program graduates, in the five-county service area, will be pleased with the education received by their employees.

Means of Program Assessment and Criteria for Success:

1a. 50% of the responding graduates of the Automotive Technology Program will report employment in the field on the Graduating Student Survey administered at the time of program completion.

1b. 80% of the graduates of the Automotive Technology Program will report employment in the field on the recent Alumni Survey administered one year after graduation.

2a. At the close of their final term, 90% of the graduates will be able to identify and correct within a given period of time all of the mechanical problems in five test cars that have been "prepared" for the students by Automotive Technology Program faculty. No single automotive malfunction will fail to be identified and corrected by more than 20% of students.

2b. 80% of Automotive Technology Program graduates will pass the National Automotive Test. On no subscale will students average missing 30% or more of the items.

3a. 80% of the respondents to an Employer Survey conducted every 3 years by the college will respond that they would be pleased to employ future graduates.

appropriate secondary criteria for success have also been identified. These criteria might have been identified in the statement of Intended Educational Outcomes.

• One of these three column examples can constitute a department's assessment plan which is the current general expectation of regional accreditation associations with the exception of the Southern Association of Colleges and Schools that requires more of its institutions based upon the longer history of implementation in that region.

Concluding Comments Regarding Assessment

In summary, several points concerning assessment should be borne in mind:

• Assessment activities should be perceived as a means toward improvement of academic programming not an end in themselves.

• Assessment results find their primary meaning in relationship to intended educational (student) outcomes.

• Assessment activities, while detailed and occasionally technical, are not beyond the grasp or comprehension of faculty when accomplished with a desirable level of simplicity.

• While faculty have a vital interest in assessment, providing the coordination and logistical support to see that assessment gets done is an administrative responsibility.

When unmasked and openly discussed, assessment is far from the threat frequently asserted. By working together and establishing a clear understanding concerning intentions, limitations, and roles, departmental faculty and administrators can establish a workable assessment program serving the interest of all concerned.

References

El-Khawas, E. (July, 1993). *Campus Trends*. Higher Education Panel No. 83. Washington, DC: American Council on Education.

Ewell, P. T. (1987). Establishing a campus-based assessment program. In D. F. Halpern (ed.), *Student Outcomes Assessment: What Institutions Stand to Gain* (pp. 9-24). San Francisco: Jossey-Bass.

Chapter IV

CLOSING THE LOOP TO SHOW USE OF ASSESSMENT RESULTS TO IMPROVE INSTRUCTIONAL PROGRAMMING

The end product of virtually all assessment activities (except some accountability initiatives) is the improvement of academic programming based upon the use of assessment results. Without being able to demonstrate such use of assessment results, all previous activities fall short of their intended purpose.

The communication of assessment results to the departmental level is the first step toward its use. The case study institutions indicated that among the least effective means of communication of assessment results to the departmental level was the forwarding of voluminous amounts of tabular data. Verbal communication of results was reported somewhat more effective than tabular presentations. However, the most effective means of communicating assessment results to faculty in academic departments was found to be in summary form with graphic support of tabular data presented orally at departmental faculty meetings (see Chapter III, *Assessment Case Studies*).

Receipt of assessment results usually initiates one of three actions by the department. First, improvement in the means of assessment or restructuring of the statement of intended educational outcomes. Second, the decision to take no curricular action based upon assessment findings indicating accomplishment of intended educational (student) outcomes. Third, utilization of the assessment data to change and improve the performance of its programs and its students.

When changes in programming were made at the case study institutions, they tended to be of two types: "what we teach" and "how we teach." Those changes related to "what we teach" included closer alignment of course offerings with the requirements of the "world of work," or restructuring of the sequence of the curriculum to lead more logically from one subject to another where appropriate. The changes reported in "How we teach" were as numerous as the departments and institutions responding to our inquiries in the preparation of *Assessment Case Studies.* In general, it was reported that different instructional techniques were being used to facilitate student learning and that the majority of these techniques (use of audiovisual aids, interactive computing, increased laboratory experiences, and increased homework) required the student to become a more active participant in the learning process.

The use of assessment results in relation to budgeting is a very complicated issue. Several regional accrediting associations (based upon their appropriate assertion that planning should drive budgeting) appear to endorse the use of assessment results as a major factor in the budgeting process. The authors urge extreme caution in this practice for several reasons. First, budgeting funds *educational processes* whereas assessment activities relate to *intended educational (student) outcomes*. Second, if assessment results are seen as a primary driving force behind the budgeting process, the <u>purpose</u> of the assessment process shifts from "improving learning" to "getting increased funding." If additional funding is not available (a likely condition on most campuses), does that "excuse" departments from improving their programs? Assessment and program improvement activities should be based upon existing departmental resources and only with great caution used to occasionally "inform" rather than drive the budgeting process.

Documentation of the use of assessment results should be planned early in the assessment process. Responsibility for maintaining this documentation is probably best lodged at the departmental level with copies forwarded for information only purposes to a central clearinghouse at the institutional level. Normally, the departmental administrator charged with implementation will also have responsibility for documentation for the use of results.

The key concepts in documentation of the use of results are to clearly relate the use back to the intended educational outcomes and to keep the documentation at a minimum of effort. The format suggested in the Assessment Record Book shown in Appendices A and B should suffice for most purposes for each academic program in the department.

Figures 13-16 depict the full "Five-Column Model" tracing development from the Expanded Statement of Institutional Purpose, through programmatic statements of Intended Educational Outcomes, as measured by specified Means of Assessment in relationship to preestablished criteria for program success and ultimately into actual Use of Results to improve programming.

Evaluating the extent of success in your adaptation of these "Five Column Models" to the academic programs within your department can be accomplished utilizing the "Dozen Questions" outline provided in Figure 17 at the close of this chapter.

The format shown in Appendix A, the Assessment Record Book, is a narrative adaptation of the graphic portrayal of this linkage shown in Figures 13-16. In order to document completely its assessment activities, each department should complete one set of assessment records annually for each academic program of the department.Forms A, B, and C provided in Appendix A and available to download from www.iea-nich.com are intended for direct usage by readers. This web location provides all forms and instructions for several popular word processing programs utilizing Microsoft Windows©. For those readers not able to utilize the www, permission to photocopy, modify, and use the forms and instructions contained in Appendix A is granted by the authors who hold the copyright on this publication. Appendix B is provided to illustrate an example of adaptation of one of the graphic representations or "Five-Column Models," as in Figure 13, to the more narrative format contained in the Assessment Record Book.

By whatever means is chosen, a clear expectation in the mind of the public and its representatives is that institutions will be able to document not only their plans for assessment, but the actual results and how these results were used to improve programming.

Figure 13

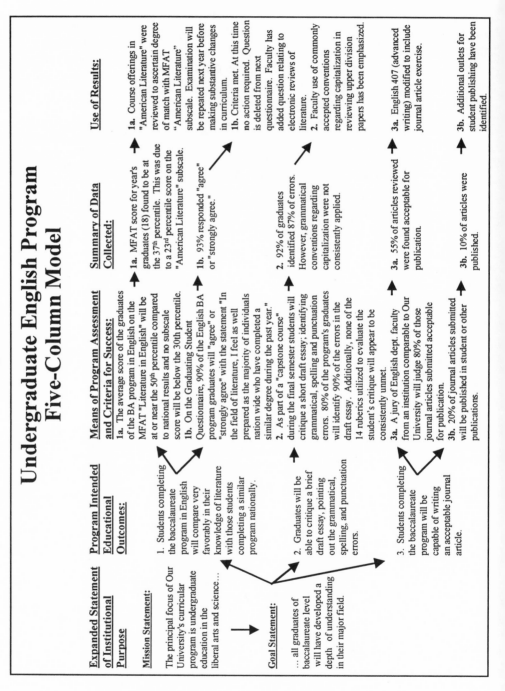

Undergraduate English Program
Five-Column Model

Expanded Statement of Institutional Purpose	Program Intended Educational Outcomes:	Means of Program Assessment and Criteria for Success:	Summary of Data Collected:	Use of Results:
Mission Statement: The principal focus of Our University's curricular program is undergraduate education in the liberal arts and science…	1. Students completing the baccalaureate program in English will compare very favorably in their knowledge of literature with those students completing a similar program nationally.	**1a.** The average score of the graduates of the BA program in English on the MFAT "Literature in English" will be at or near the 50th percentile compared to national results and no subscale score will be below the 30th percentile. **1b.** On the Graduating Student Questionnaire, 90% of the English BA program graduates will "agree" or "strongly agree" with the statement "In the field of literature, I feel as well prepared as the majority of individuals nation wide who have completed a similar degree during the past year."	**1a.** MFAT score for year's graduates (18) found to be at the 37th percentile. This was due to a 23rd percentile score on the "American Literature" subscale. **1b.** 93% responded "agree" or "strongly agree."	**1a.** Course offerings in "American Literature" were reviewed to ascertain degree of match with MFAT "American Literature" subscale. Examination will be repeated next year before making substantive changes in curriculum. **1b.** Criteria met. At this time no action required. Question is deleted from next questionnaire. Faculty has added question relating to electronic reviews of literature.
Goal Statement: … all graduates of baccalaureate level will have developed a depth of understanding in their major field.	2. Graduates will be able to critique a brief draft essay, pointing out the grammatical, spelling, and punctuation errors.	**2.** As part of a "capstone course" during the final semester students will critique a short draft essay; identifying grammatical, spelling and punctuation errors. 80% of the program's graduates will identify 90% of the errors in the draft essay. Additionally, none of the 14 ruberics utilized to evaluate the student's critique will appear to be consistently unmet.	**2.** 92% of graduates identified 87% of errors. However, grammatical conventions regarding capitalization were not consistently applied.	**2.** Faculty use of commonly accepted conventions regarding capitalization in reviewing upper division papers has been emphasized.
	3. Students completing the baccalaureate program will be capable of writing an acceptable journal article.	**3a.** A jury of English dept. faculty from an institution comparable to Our University will judge 80% of those journal articles submitted acceptable for publication. **3b.** 20% of journal articles submitted will be published in student or other publications.	**3a.** 55% of articles reviewed were found acceptable for publication. **3b.** 10% of articles were published.	**3a.** English 407 (advanced writing) modified to include journal article exercise. **3b.** Additional outlets for student publishing have been identified.

Figure 14

Accounting Degree Program
Five-Column Model

Expanded Statement of Institutional Purpose / Mission Statement / Goal Statement	Program Intended Educational Outcomes:	Means of Program Assessment and Criteria for Success:	Summary of Data Collected:	Use of Results:
Expanded Statement of Institutional Purpose	1. Students completing the baccalaureate program in accounting will be well prepared for their first position in the field.	1a. 80% of accounting majors taking the CPA exam will pass at least three of four parts on the exam. Further, the rate of passage on any single part will not be less than 80%.	1a. 72% of those taking the CPA exam passed all four parts. 97% passed three of four parts. Only 74% passed the auditing portion.	1a. Methods of teaching auditing revised by faculty to provide more case studies.
Mission Statement:		1b. Employers of accounting program graduates hired through Our University Placement Service will indicate on a survey forwarded to them by the Placement Service one year after employment of the graduate, no less than a 7.5 overall average (on a scale of 1-10) on their evaluation of the ten critical accounting skills exhibited by the graduate. No individual skill rating will be less than an average of 5.0.	1b. Average rating of 8.3 was recorded. However, the critical skill "ability to work with clients" received an average evaluation of 4.2.	1b. Accountant/Client relations practicum integrated into Accounting 428.
The principal focus of Our University's curricular program is undergraduate education in the liberal arts and sciences....	2. Baccalaureate graduates of the accounting program will find ready employment in the field.	2a. Career Center will report 90% of accounting graduates registered each fall received a job offer by the close of spring semester.	2a. 73% received a job offer.	2a. Accounting "Job Fair" has been scheduled mid-spring semester to boost early employment.
Goal Statement:		2b. 60% of students completing the accounting degree program will indicate that they are currently employed or have accepted a job offer in their response to Our University's Graduating Student Survey.	2b. 80 % indicated receipt of job offer.	2b. Criterion on Graduating Student Survey raised to 80%.
All graduates of baccalaureate programs will have developed a depth of understanding in their major field....	3. Graduates will be experienced in the use of personal computers for accounting procedures	3a. Graduates will be required during their last semester to complete successfully (as judged by a jury of faculty from the department), a major accounting project utilizing personal computer applications. 80% of the projects will be judged acceptable on first review.	3a. 63% of graduates' computer applications were judged acceptable on first review by faculty panel.	3a. More personal computer applications were integrated into core accounting classes (101, 103, etc.).
		3b. 75% of accounting graduates will indicate on Graduating Student Questionnaire that they "agree" or "strongly agree" with the statement "I feel very comfortable utilizing a personal computer for accounting".	3b. 81% indicated "agree" or "strongly agree."	3b. No action required. Will change item next cycle.

Figure 15

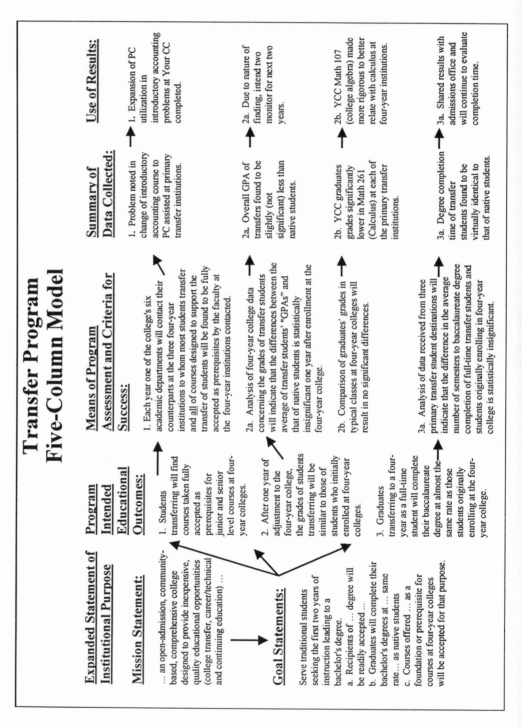

Transfer Program
Five-Column Model

Expanded Statement of Institutional Purpose

Mission Statement:

… an open-admission, community-based, comprehensive college designed to provide inexpensive, quality educational opportunities (college transfer, career/technical and continuing education) …

Goal Statements:

Serve traditional students seeking the first two years of instruction leading to a bachelor's degree.
a. Recipients of … degree will be readily accepted …
b. Graduates will complete their bachelor's degrees at … same rate… as native students
c. Courses offered … as a foundation or prerequisite for courses at four-year colleges will be accepted for that purpose.

Program Intended Educational Outcomes:

1. Students transferring will find courses taken fully accepted as prerequisites for junior and senior level courses at four-year colleges.

2. After one year of adjustment to the four-year college, the grades of students transferring will be similar to those of students who initially enrolled at four-year colleges.

3. Graduates transferring to a four-year as a full-time student will complete their baccalaureate degree at almost the same rate as those students originally enrolling at the four-year college.

Means of Program Assessment and Criteria for Success:

1. Each year one of the college's six academic departments will contact their counterparts at the three four-year institutions to whom most students transfer and all of courses designed to support the transfer of students will be found to be fully accepted as prerequisites by the faculty at the four-year institutions contacted.

2a. Analysis of four-year college data concerning the grades of transfer students will indicate that the differences between the average of transfer students' "GPAs" and that of native students is statistically insignificant one year after enrollment at the four-year college.

2b. Comparison of graduates' grades in typical classes at four-year colleges will result in no significant differences.

3a. Analysis of data received from three primary transfer student destinations will indicate that the difference in the average number of semesters to baccalaureate degree completion of full-time transfer students and students originally enrolling in four-year college is statistically insignificant.

Summary of Data Collected:

1. Problem noted in change of introductory accounting course to PC assisted at primary transfer institutions.

2a. Overall GPA of transfers found to be slightly (not significant) less than native students.

2b. YCC graduates grades significantly lower in Math 261 (Calculus) at each of the primary transfer institutions.

3a. Degree completion time of transfer students found to be virtually identical to that of native students.

Use of Results:

1. Expansion of PC utilization in introductory accounting problems at Your CC completed.

2a. Due to nature of finding, intend two monitor for next two years.

2b. YCC Math 107 (college algebra) made more rigorous to better relate with calculus at four-year institutions.

3a. Shared results with admissions office and will continue to evaluate completion time.

Figure 16

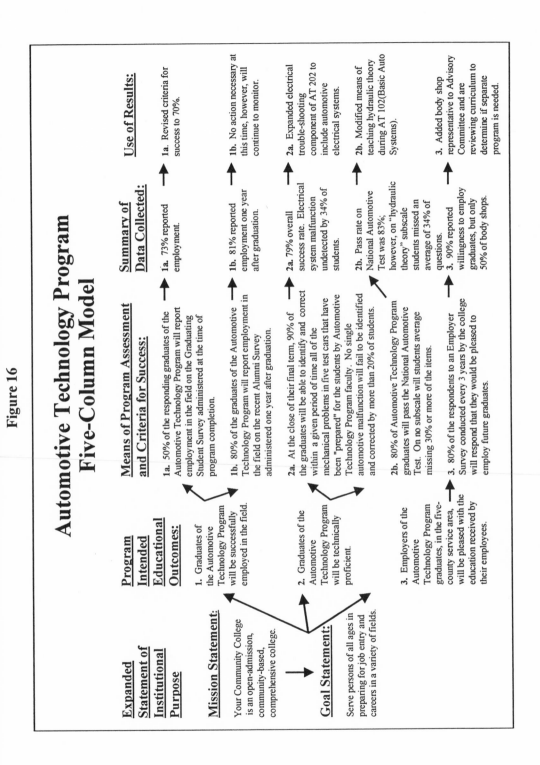

Automotive Technology Program Five-Column Model

Expanded Statement of Institutional Purpose

Mission Statement:

Your Community College is an open-admission, community-based, comprehensive college.

Goal Statement:

Serve persons of all ages in preparing for job entry and careers in a variety of fields.

Program Intended Educational Outcomes:

1. Graduates of the Automotive Technology Program will be successfully employed in the field.

2. Graduates of the Automotive Technology Program will be technically proficient.

3. Employers of the Automotive Technology Program graduates, in the five-county service area, will be pleased with the education received by their employees.

Means of Program Assessment and Criteria for Success:

1a. 50% of the responding graduates of the Automotive Technology Program will report employment in the field on the Graduating Student Survey administered at the time of program completion.

1b. 80% of the graduates of the Automotive Technology Program will report employment in the field on the recent Alumni Survey administered one year after graduation.

2a. At the close of their final term, 90% of the graduates will be able to identify and correct within a given period of time all of the mechanical problems in five test cars that have been "prepared" for the students by Automotive Technology Program faculty. No single automotive malfunction will fail to be identified and corrected by more than 20% of students.

2b. 80% of Automotive Technology Program graduates will pass the National Automotive Test. On no subscale will students average missing 30% or more of the items.

3. 80% of the respondents to an Employer Survey conducted every 3 years by the college will respond that they would be pleased to employ future graduates.

Summary of Data Collected:

1a. 73% reported employment.

1b. 81% reported employment one year after graduation.

2a. 79% overall success rate. Electrical system malfunction undetected by 34% of students.

2b. Pass rate on National Automotive Test was 83%; however, on "hydraulic theory" subscale students missed an average of 34% of questions.

3. 90% reported willingness to employ graduates, but only 50% of body shops.

Use of Results:

1a. Revised criteria for success to 70%.

1b. No action necessary at this time, however, will continue to monitor.

2a. Expanded electrical trouble-shooting component of AT 202 to include automotive electrical systems.

2b. Modified means of teaching hydraulic theory during AT 102(Basic Auto Systems).

3. Added body shop representative to Advisory Committee and are reviewing curriculum to determine if separate program is needed.

Figure 17

**A DOZEN QUESTIONS TO CONSIDER WHEN
REVIEWING INSTRUCTIONAL ASSESSMENT REPORTS**

Relationship to Institutional Level

1.   Is support of the institution's statement of purpose established?

Program Intended Educational Outcomes

2.   Are the statements of intended educational (student) outcomes limited to three to five?

3.   Are the statements of intended outcomes clear and concise containing only one concept for measurement (as opposed to more "bundled" outcomes often separated by commas, semi-colons, or conjunctions)?

4.   Are the statements all formulated in terms of what the graduates or program completers as a group will be able to think, know, or do?

Means of Program Assessment and Criteria for Success

5.   Do the means of assessment referenced measure the accomplishment of the intended outcomes described?

6.   Do the means of assessment seem feasible and appropriate given the time and resources available?

7.   Are multiple means of assessment utilized in most cases?

8.   Is a criteria for program success established for each means of assessment?

Summary of Data Collected

9.   Are sufficient data provided in the summary of assessment results to convince the reader that the assessment described actually took place?

10.   Are the assessment results analyzed in such a way as to focus on the accomplishment of the intended outcomes cited?

Use of Results

11.   Is there evidence of broad scale faculty involvement in determination of the use of results for program improvement?

12.   Do the use of results flow from and relate to the intended outcomes and assessment results?

Chapter V

Assessment in Graduate and Professional Degree Programs

The initial emphasis of assessment activities at most campuses is on their undergraduate programs. This is so because the primary (though not exclusive) focus of regional accrediting requirements concerns undergraduate programs. Also, from a practical point of view, assessment of graduate and professional programs is considerably easier based upon the experience gained in assessment at the undergraduate level.

Intended Educational (Student) Outcomes in Graduate and Professional Programs

Because of the more advanced nature of these programs and the reduced breadth of their curricula, intended educational outcomes tend to be focused on the following topics regarding each field:

- Advanced knowledge
- Acquisition of professional level skills
- Attainment of licensure
- Ability to do research
- Contributions through original research (Doctoral programs primarily)
- Employment
- Teaching ability at the collegiate level

Means of Assessment in Graduate and Professional Level Programs

The assessment of advanced knowledge in graduate and professional level programs is significantly complicated by the absence of standardized commercially developed testing for such programs. However, it is enhanced by the existence of summary comprehensive written and oral examinations as well as licensure examinations. Doctoral and Masters programs having either written or oral comprehensive examinations as part of the students' normal matriculation already may have captured most of the information necessary for assessment. Refer to the "column and row matrix" Figure 8 (see page 43) and consider the "criteria" referenced there to be the individual questions or groups of questions on each program's comprehensive examinations. Re-analysis of the data "across the rows" to reflect program assessment (rather than as earlier down the columns to determine if the individual student passed the examination) quickly yields a significant amount of exceedingly useful assessment information. This is exemplified in Figure 18 on the following page.

Those professional programs focused upon graduates' licensure (medicine, law, dentistry, architecture, counseling, psychology, etc.) can profit greatly from the incorporation of such feedback into the assessment process for those programs. The key to the utilization of this information for assessment purposes is the provision of not only pass/fail rates, but also scale scores for the different parts of the licensure examination. These scale scores enable the institution to focus upon improvements in particular components of its curriculum (See Figure 14, page 55, for an example of this at the undergraduate level).

Common to virtually all Graduate and Professional Programs is the completion of some type of thesis, dissertation or project. Such examples of graduates' work provide a ready and ideal means for assessment of their ability to do research, perform an advanced skill, or produce writing of a technical nature. In most cases, such ideal opportunities for assessment are under utilized. Application of the "column and row matrix" illustrated in Figure 8, page 43 to quickly exploit this opportunity and provide immediately available assessment information for program is suggested.

In professional (and to a lesser extent graduate) level programs, employer and practicum/ internship supervisor observations can be readily incorporated into the assessment process. In many programs, such individual student evaluation is already in existence. The grading criteria upon which various observers (practicum/internship supervisors, etc.) are asked to base their evaluation form the rows of the "column and row matrix" referenced above and can be quickly related to the intended outcomes of the program. Surveys of employers can also be used in a similar manner.

Assessment at the Masters and Doctoral levels each exhibit some unique characteristics. In Masters programs, it is not uncommon to find intended outcomes relating to the proportion of graduates applying for further study at the Doctoral level that were accepted. Some Masters programs are even found to identify graduate acceptance to particular Doctoral programs as constituting their intended outcome. At the Doctoral level and in some professional programs, numbers of contributions to the scholarly literature in the field such as papers published in refereed journals or presented at national/ regional meetings are often utilized as a convenient form of assessment. Assessment of students' ability to teach is frequently focused on classroom, peer, and faculty evaluation procedures common at many institutions of higher learning.

Figure 18

Doctorate in Literature
Five-Column Model

Expanded Statement of Institutional Purpose	Program Intended Educational Outcomes:	Means of Program Assessment and Criteria for Success:	Summary of Data Collected:	Use of Results:
Mission Statement: Our University offers masters and doctoral degree programs in selected areas that will prepare individuals for positions of leadership in their chosen careers.	**1.** Graduates will demonstrate a depth of knowledge in one of six specializations.	**1a.** Each year 80% will pass the comprehensive exam on their first attempt.	**1a.** This year 9 of 10 students passed the comprehensive on their first attempt. Only two specializations tested.	**1a.** While choice of specialization will be continued, faculty discussing "breadth" requirement.
		1b. Over the past three years, the pass rate in each specialization will be at least 70%.	**1b.** Over the last three years, four of seven students in American Literature specialization passed on first testing.	**1b.** Contemporary American Writers (Eng. 755) now required of all in American Literature specialization.
Goal Statement: Although the primary thrust of Our University will continue to be its undergraduate program of instruction, graduate education and research will play an increasing role in support of the institution and its attraction and retention of outstanding students and faculty.	**2.** Graduates will exhibit strong literary analysis skills.	**2a.** 50% of the graduates will have a review of literary work accepted for publication.	**2a.** Two of graduates (20%) had such works accepted for publication.	**2a.** Requirements for students to submit publishable literary analysis for faculty review throughout program now more fully enforced.
		2b. Virtually all of the dissertations reviewed will meet departmental requirements for literary analysis.	**2b.** All (8) dissertations were found to meet departmental requirements for literary analysis.	**2b.** Departmental rubrics for literary analysis revised for more rigor.
	3. Graduates will be highly competitive in the college teaching market.	**3a.** Course evaluations in classes taught by students will exceed departmental, college and university averages.	**3a.** Of the ten graduates, three found to exceed department and college averages. None, however, equaled university norms.	**3a.** University instructional development seminar now required in students' first semester of graduate level enrollment.
		3b. 80% of graduates reached by phone one year after graduation will report employment in field teaching at a college or university.	**3b.** One year after graduation 40% (four) of last year's doctoral graduates (ten) reported employment in field teaching at college level.	**3b.** Improved publication record (2a) and instructional skills (3a) required should lead to improved employment rate.

Concluding Comments

Requirements by professional accrediting associations increasingly influence assessment in such fields. The information prepared for satisfaction of professional association assessment requirements will, in many cases, suffice for regional accreditation purposes. However, professional accreditation itself is a validation of the program's *educational process* and **not** its *outcomes*. Hence, the professional accreditation of a program is not a valid means of outcome assessment.

The five-column model shown in Figure 18 is representative of implementation in graduate and professional level programming. However, the richness and variety of these fields defies any stereotypical example.

Chapter VI

GENERAL EDUCATION: THE SINGLE GREATEST ASSESSMENT ISSUE

On almost any campus (two-year, four-year, public, or private) that offers undergraduate education, assessment in the General Education program will be found to be the most complex, controversial, and furthest behind. This important element of the educational process serves as the foundation for the degree programs or majors at the institution as depicted in Figure 19. General Education is usually composed of approximately 24 to 56 semester

Figure 19

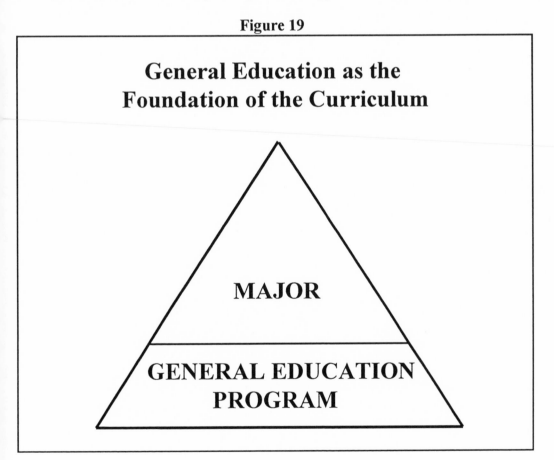

General Education as the
Foundation of the Curriculum

MAJOR

GENERAL EDUCATION
PROGRAM

hours taken primarily during the freshman and sophomore years at four-year institutions and in the transfer curricula at two-year colleges. However, between 6 and 12 hours of General Education is also found in occupational/technical programming leading to the associate degree.

In most instances, General Education is laden with a number of issues making curriculum development and assessment exceedingly difficult. The wide variety of opinions concerning the intended educational outcomes of a General Education program forms the basis for a good portion of this controversy. However, the legitimately subjective or value oriented nature of some of the intended educational outcomes which are typical of General Education also complicates the matter. On another level, General Education becomes highly inflammatory on many campuses because the nature of the curriculum requires cross-departmental cooperation in which the institution has not recently been engaged. Further, because the connection between General Education requirements (taken by larger numbers of students) and the courses necessary to support those requirements (and employee faculty) is so evident, "turf protection" becomes the hallmark of most General Education discussions.

There are two basic approaches to curriculum development and assessment of General Education. The first of these approaches deals with the concept of General Education as a whole. However, it acknowledges the contribution of separate disciplines such as communications, mathematics, humanities, behavioral and social science, natural science, etc. This approach usually fits well with regional accreditation requirements and is more easily adapted to assessment activities. The second approach (unfortunately the most common), lacks such central thrust or core identification of General Education skills, abilities or values. It is composed of a collection of courses as a portion of "distribution requirements" loosely agreed upon by highly independent departments and collectively described in the institution's catalogue. This approach is the most common because it avoids the necessary value judgments regarding the importance of these courses and minimizes institutional conflict (as well as some would say this educational process). This latter course of curriculum development in General Education does not fit well with most regional accreditation expectations and assuredly is not prone to facilitate an institution's assessment efforts. This approach leads departments such as English, Math, History, etc. to implement some type of *course-based* assessment procedures for their many service courses. Ordinarily, this results in a number of uncoordinated assessment activities, which are both burdensome and often ineffective. While attractive from a campus political perspective, this is an approach that leads many General Education assessment efforts to "choke and die". While challenging, approaching General Education curriculum development and assessment as a whole is in the long run much more preferable.

Intended General Education (Student) Outcomes

General Education (student) outcomes are frequently described in terms of students':

- Capabilities in reading, writing, speaking, listening, abstract inquiry, critical thinking or logical reasoning
- Understanding of numerical data, scientific inquiry, global issues, historical perspective, and literary or philosophical perspective
- Development of ethical perspective and cultural diversity issues
- Appreciation of the fine and performing arts

Characteristic of General Education are those valid outcomes which some would describe as "truth and beauty" statements, such as those referenced above concerning abstract inquiry, critical thinking, logical reasoning, ethical perspective, cultural diversity, and appreciation of the fine and performing arts. These concepts, while less finite and "measurable" than skills in reading, writing, and the understanding of numerical data and scientific inquiry, are none the less important cornerstones of our society and warrant continuation in the face of assessment challenges. However, each will also require careful refinement to operational terminology more subject to assessment.

It is important that each academic department review the institution's General Education outcomes and be prepared to play either a key or supporting role in their assessment. However, just as in the major, the General Education *program* should develop its own long list of intended educational outcomes and from that list select a more reasonable number of between three (3) and five (5) intended outcomes for assessment during any one time period.

In identifying General Education intended outcomes, institutions are faced with a choice of either breadth or depth. A choice in favor of *breadth* would feature one outcome each relating to a number of different fields such as reading, writing, speaking, numerical data, or ethical perspective. Under this approach, many of the disciplinary components of the institution would be involved to a limited degree in assessment of General Education each year. On the other hand, an institution may choose the *depth* approach in any year and have all three to five outcomes related to one field. Under this approach, most other disciplines at the institution would not be involved with General Education assessment during that particular year. However, the field selected would be extensively involved. The point is that under either approach *some disciplines may not be involved in assessment of General Education during a particular year*, but will become involved either intensively or at a moderate level in the following year. This does not prohibit those disciplines not involved directly in program level general education assessment from conducting their own independent classroom assessment activities. However, it legitimizes their temporary absence from program level General Education assessment endeavors.

Means of Assessment of Intended General Education (Student) Outcomes

Assessment of General Education normally transpires at the end of the first two years for Baccalaureate program students and at roughly the same period of time for transfer students at two-year colleges. Four-year institutions will want to assure that they receive neither "the credit nor the blame" for the General Education received by students transferring to them from two-year colleges. Hence, they will want to identify those students and separately analyze their General Educational assessment results.

Just as in the case of the major, assessment of General Education is possible utilizing either locally developed or standardized means of assessment. Locally developed means of General Education assessment in the cognitive area are seldom comprehensive in nature and usually cover little past the basic skills of writing and mathematics. In these disciplines, some form of a writing sample is usually drawn for analysis by the faculty and a locally developed mathematics exam is either separately administered or included as a common examination in the most demanding math courses students are required to complete. Thus, the use of locally developed means of assessment usually fails to cover many of what can be described as the "higher order" General Education outcomes.

Standardized means of General Education assessment include the *Collegiate Assessment of Academic Proficiency (CAAP), Academic Profile,* or *College Basic Academic Subjects Exam (CBASE).* While each of these examinations represents a substantial improvement over that previously available, most faculty will find none of them to fit the General Education curriculum at their institution. However, all of these examinations do benefit from (a) being comprehensive in nature, (b) ready availability, and (c) the provision of a normative reference group. As a means of facilitating discussion of General Education assessment, these authors can think of little better activity than bringing all three of the referenced standardized assessment examinations onto campus for review. (See Chapters III and IV of a *Practitioner's Handbook for Institutional Effectiveness and Student Outcomes Assessment).*

The use of attitudinal assessment concerning the General Education program is frequently overlooked as a potential means of assessment. Much usable information can be gained from graduate attitudes toward what they learned during their General Education program; however, this type of information described as "indirect" is best used to confirm other assessment results.

Frequently, more subjective or value laden intended outcomes in General Education are only assessable based upon graduates' actions once they have left the institution. Faculty should identify actions later in life that would be typical of values such as a commitment to religion, the enjoyment of reading, or the desire to participate in the democratic process. An alumni survey can then be utilized to determine the frequency of such actions (church attendance, reading patterns, voting record, etc.) among graduates.

Another often overlooked source of General Education assessment information is the opinion of employers concerning the skills of the institution's graduates. In case after case, employers cite General Education skills and values as greater deficiencies than knowledge or skills directly related to their employee's major in college.

Finally, substantial evidence may be gained from performance type assessment measures in General Education. Included in the General Education example provided, Figure 20, is the utilization of a writing sample in which students are asked to perform the act of writing (as opposed to knowing grammar and writing concepts) as a means of assessment of General Education. Additionally, performance assessment regarding oral communication skills through the use of videotape is frequently encountered. The case study approach observing the performance of students placed in circumstances in which they are asked to demonstrate certain values intended as part of the General Education curriculum is also practiced.

Use of Results in General Education

The use of assessment results regarding General Education is even more difficult than in the major because of the substantial vested interest involved on the part of many relatively independent faculty and departments. Change can be expected to take several years to negotiate and put in place. The results of those changes will take even more time to show results of the improvements made. Finally, the changes made based upon assessment results can be expected to be evolutionary refinements rather than frequently publicized more revolutionary or radical changes.

Concluding Comments Regarding Assessment in General Education

Each department offering a substantial number of service courses plays an important role within the assessment and improvement of General Education. However, no department operates in this arena independent of other departments. It is essential that the institution approach General Education as a whole or program and that each department play its own important and unique role in the improvement of this critical part of the institution's curriculum.

Figure 20

General Education Program Five-Column Model

Expanded Statement of Institutional Purpose	Program Intended Educational Outcomes:	Means of Program Assessment and Criteria for Success:	Summary of Data Collected:	Use of Results:
Mission: The principle focus of Our University's curricular program is undergraduate education in the liberal arts….	**1.** Students will compose an acceptable essay concerning a current events topic assigned using Standard Written English (SWE).	**1a.** Students' composite scores on the written essay portion of the ACT(CAAP) will average 4.2 or more on their 6.0 scale.	**1a.** Average score of those tested in the Spring Semester was 4.4 on the Essay scale of ACT(CAAP).	**1a.** Criteria met. No action required. Will continue assessment next year.
		1b. 75% of those writing samples chosen will pass the written standards rubric with no individual field score less than 3.0 on a 5.0 scale as judged by a panel of English department faculty.	**1b.** 82% of writing sample passed with no individual field score less than 3.0. The "thematic organization" scores were substantially lower than other scale scores.	**1b.** English Composition 102 modified to emphasize "thematic organization."
Goals: Graduates will: **a.** Express themselves clearly in writing. **b.** Make an effective verbal presentation. **c.** Read and analyze periodical literature. **d.** Complete accurately basic mathematical calculations. **e.** Demonstrate a commitment to Judeo-Christian beliefs.	**2.** Students will demonstrate the ability to accomplish basic mathematical processes through the level of college algebra.	**2.** The mean score on the "Algebra" sub-scale of the ACT (CAAP) will be 15.0 or more.	**2.** Average score on the ACT(CAAP) "Algebra" sub-scale was 13.07.	**2.** Mathematics faculty are reviewing the items on the "Algebra" sub-scale.
	3. Graduates will act in such a way to show their commitment to Judeo-Christian beliefs.	**3a.** When faced with a moral dilemma as part of the case study required in each majors capstone course, 80% of graduating class will choose the solution identified by the faculty as that demonstrating a commitment to Judeo-Christian beliefs.	**3a.** 78% of students chose the appropriate solution to the moral dilemma posed. However, those majoring in Business and Pre-Med. scored significantly less.	**3a.** Business and Pre-Med. revised curricula to integrate material linking their field with the institutional commitment to Judeo-Christian beliefs.
		3b. The average monthly attendance at church reported on the recent alumni survey will exceed 2.5 times per month each academic year.	**3b.** Average church attendance reported on the last three surveys has fallen to 1.73 days per month.	**3b.** Student Life integrated more denominationally related activities into dormitory programming and social functions.

ASSESSMENT RECORD BOOK FORMS AND INSTRUCTIONS FOR COMPLETION

The "Instructions for Completion of Assessment Record Book forms for Instructional Programs" as well as the Forms A, B, and C, shown in succession on the following pages may be downloaded into several popular word processing programs utilizing Microsoft Windows © from www.iea-nich.com. For those readers not able to utilize the www, permission to photocopy, modify, and use the instructions and forms contained in this appendix is granted.

INSTRUCTIONS FOR COMPLETION OF ASSESSMENT RECORD BOOK FORMS FOR INSTRUCTIONAL PROGRAMS

Instructions for Title Page (Form A)

- In the blank provided at the top of the page, *indicate the name of the academic department submitting the report*. There should be one Assessment Record Book for each academic department on campus that offers a major.
- In the blank provided, *indicate the "Assessment Period Covered" by the report that follows*. This should be indicated in months and years. For example: July 2000 – June 2001.
- In the space provided, *enter the date the assessment report was forwarded to the committee or individual responsible for assessment at the institution*. This will assist in identification of each iteration and potential refinements of the assessment report covering the same time period.
- On the space provided under "Title of Instructional Degree Programs," *list this department's degree programs scheduled for reporting as listed in the institution's catalogue*.
- In the space provided, *list the "Degree Level"* of each of the programs listed on the left. For example, if the institution offers a bachelors and a master's degree in English both degree levels would be listed.
- In the blank provided, *enter the name of the individual who was responsible for the report*. In some cases an individual staff member in the department has been identified to represent the department in assessment matters and that person would sign the form, otherwise the Department Chair would sign the form.

Instructions for Linkage Page (Form B)

- The four blanks at the top of the page should have the *identical information as provided on the Title Page (Form A)*. Each "Instructional Degree Program" will have a

Form B and one Form C for each "Intended Educational (Student) Outcome" listed on the Form B.

- In the box identified as "Institutional Mission Reference," *enter all or a portion of the institutional mission that is supported by the instructional degree program.* For some institutions this may not be available.
- In the box containing "College/University Goal(s) Supported," identify which of the institution's goals this instructional program directly supports.
- In each of the blocks listed under "Intended Educational (Student) Outcomes," *enter one of the intended educational (student) outcomes for the instructional degree program listed above.* It is recommended that there be at least three of these intended educational (student) outcomes and definitely no more than five.

Instructions for Intended Educational (Student) Outcome Report Pages (Form C)

- You will have one Intended Educational (Student) Outcomes Report Page (Form C) for each Intended Educational (Student) Outcome stated on Form B. Thus, if there are three "Intended Educational (Student) Outcomes" listed on the Form B, there will be three Form Cs.
- The three blanks on the top of each Form C will be *completed identically to those on Form B.*
- On your first Intended Educational (Student) Outcome Sheet (Form C), in the box underneath "Intended Educational (Student) Outcome" *transfer the first outcome from Form B.* On the second Form C transfer the second Intended Educational (Student) Outcome from Form B into the box at the top of Form C, and continue this process for all outcomes.
- Complete the boxes under the "First Means of Assessment for Outcome Identified Above" subsection according to the directions listed below:
  1. Means of Program Assessment & Criteria for Success: *Describe the source of your assessment information.* (For example: practicum supervisor's report, senior project, graduating student survey, or Major Field test). Based on the selected means of assessment, provide a criterion for success which answers the question: "If our instructional program is functioning the way we think it 'ought' to function, what will be our score on this means of assessment?"
  2. Summary of Assessment Data Collected: Enter *a brief summary of the data you collected from your assessment activities.* There should be enough data here to convince the reader that assessment has been done. Data should be in exact figures, not rounded. Make sure the data collected relate back to the intended educational (student) outcome described in the first box.
  3. Use of Results to Improve Instructional Program: *Describe how the faculty of that degree program used information obtained from the assessment activities* described in the "Means of Program Assessment and Criteria for Success" block to improve the learning on the part of their students. Often, this will lead to some sort of curricular change. This improvement needs to relate back to the Intended Educational (Student) Outcome stated in the box at the top of the page. If the instructional degree program fails to meet its criteria for success then this section is used to describe what actions the faculty of the degree program have taken to assure that the intended outcome is met.
- Complete the boxes under "Second Means of Assessment for Outcomes Identified Above."

ASSESSMENT RECORD FOR
DEPARTMENT
OF

(Academic Department Name)

(Assessment Period Covered)   **(Date Submitted)**

Includes Assessment Reports for those Instructional Programs listed below:

Title of Instructional Degree Program

Degree Level
(Associate, Bachelors,
Masters, etc.)

_____ _____

_____ _____

_____ _____

_____ _____

_____ _____

_____ _____

_____ _____

_____ _____

Submitted By: _____

(Departmental Chair or Faculty Assessment Representative)

Form A

ASSESSMENT REPORT
FOR

_____   _____
(Instructional Degree Program)   (Degree Level)

_____   _____
(Assessment Period Covered)   (Date Submitted)

Expanded Statement of Institutional Purpose Linkage:

Institutional Mission Reference:

College/University Goal(s) Supported:

Intended Educational (Student) Outcomes:

1.

2.

3.

4.

5.

Form B

ASSESSMENT REPORT
FOR

_____
(Instructional Degree Program)

_____
(Degree Level)

_____
(Assessment Period Covered)

_____
(Date Submitted)

Intended Educational (Student) Outcome:

NOTE: There should be one form C for each intended outcome listed on form B. Intended outcome should be restated in the box immediately below and the intended outcome number entered in the blank spaces.

____

First Means of Assessment for Outcome Identified Above:

____a. Means of Program Assessment & Criteria for Success:

____a. Description of Data Collection & Assessment Results:

____a. Use of Results to Improve Instructional Program:

Second Means of Assessment for Outcome Identified Above:

____b. Means of Program Assessment & Criteria for Success:

____b. Description of Data Collection & Assessment Results:

____b. Use of Results to Improve Instructional Program:

Form C

EXAMPLE ENTRY IN THE ASSESSMENT RECORD BOOK FOR UNDERGRADUATE ENGLISH PROGRAM FIVE COLUMN EXAMPLE PROVIDED IN FIGURE 13

Appendix B includes a set of Assessment Record Forms completed for the Undergraduate English Program at Our University, which is Figure 13 (page 54) in this publication. Shown on Form A are all of the instructional degree programs offered by the English Department. On Form B, the specific Undergraduate English Program is related to the Mission and Goals for the institution and the intended educational outcomes are listed in the boxes 1, 2, and 3. Note that there are three completed form C's in the example provided—one for each educational outcome listed at the bottom of Form B for the Undergraduate English Program. The completed sample form C's relate each educational outcome, means of assessment and criteria for success, actual assessment results, and the use of assessment results in this example.

ASSESSMENT RECORD FOR
DEPARTMENT
OF

English
(Academic Department Name)

September 2000-August 2001
(Assessment Period Covered)

September 15, 2001
(Date Submitted)

Includes Assessment Reports for those Instructional Programs listed below:

Title of Instructional Degree Program

Degree Level
(Associate, Bachelors, Masters, etc.)

Undergraduate English Program

Bachelor of Arts

English Literature

Masters of Arts

English as a Foreign Language

Masters of Arts

_____

_____

_____

_____

_____

_____

_____

_____

Submitted By: _____
(Departmental Chair or Faculty Assessment Representative)

Form A

75

ASSESSMENT REPORT
FOR

English Program
(Instructional Degree Program)

Bachelor of Arts
(Degree Level)

September 2000-August 2001
(Assessment Period Covered)

September 15, 2001
(Date Submitted)

Expanded Statement of Institutional Purpose Linkage:

Institutional Mission Reference: The principal focus of Our University's curricular program is undergraduate education in the liberal arts and science...

College/University Goal(s) Supported: ... all graduates of baccalaureate level will have developed a depth of understanding in their major field.

Intended Educational (Student) Outcomes:

1. Students completing the baccalaureate program in English will compare very favorably in their knowledge of literature with those students completing a similar program nationally.

2. Graduates will be able to critique a brief draft essay, pointing out the grammatical, spelling, and punctuation errors.

3. Students completing the baccalaureate program will be capable of writing an acceptable journal article.

4.

5.

Form B

ASSESSMENT REPORT
FOR

English Program

(Instructional Degree Program)

Bachelor of Arts

(Degree Level)

September 2000-August 2001

(Period Covered)

September 15, 2001

(Date Submitted)

Intended Educational (Student) Outcome:

NOTE: There should be one form C for each intended outcome listed on form B. Intended outcome should be restated in the box immediately below and the intended outcome number entered in the blank spaces.

1. Students completing the baccalaureate program in English will compare very favorably in their knowledge of literature with those students completing a similar program nationally.

First Means of Assessment for Outcome Identified Above:

_1 a. Means of Program Assessment and Criteria for Success: The average score of the graduates of the BA program in English on the MFAT "Literature in English" will be at or near the 50th percentile compared to national results, and no sub-scale score will be below the 30th percentile.

_1 a. Summary of Assessment Data Collected: MFAT score for year's graduates (18) found to be at the 37th percentile. This was due to the 23rd percentile score on "American Literature" scale.

_1 a. Use of Results to Improve Instructional Program: Course offerings in "American Literature" being reviewed to ascertain degree of match with MFAT "American Literature" scale. Examination will be repeated next year before making substantive changes in curriculum.

Second Means of Assessment for Outcome Identified Above:

_1 b. Means of Program Assessment & Criteria for Success: 90% of the English BA program graduates will "agree" or "strongly agree" with the statement; "In the field of literature, I feel as well prepared as the majority of individuals nation wide who have completed a similar degree during the past year."

_1 b. Summary of Assessment Data Collected: 93% responded "agree" or "strongly agree."

_1 b. Use of Results to Improve Instructional Program: Criteria met. At this time no action required. Question is deleted from next questionnaire. Faculty has added question related to electronic reviews of Literature.

Form C

ASSESSMENT REPORT
FOR

English Program	*Bachelor of Arts*
(Instructional Degree Program)	(Degree Level)

September 2000-August 2001	September 15, 2001
(Period Covered)	(Date Submitted)

Intended Educational (Student) Outcome:

NOTE: There should be one form C for each intended outcome listed on form B. Intended outcome should be restated in the box immediately below and the intended outcome number entered in the blank spaces.

2. Graduates will be able to critique a brief draft essay, pointing out the grammatical, spelling, and punctuation errors.

First Means of Assessment for Outcome Identified Above:

_2 a. Means of Program Assessment & Criteria for Success: As part of a "capstone course" during the final semester students will critique a short draft essay; identifying grammatical, spelling and punctuation errors. 80% of the program's graduates will identify 90% of the errors in draft essay. Additionally, none of the 14 ruberics utilized to evaluate the student's critique will appear to be consistently unmet.

_2 a. Summary of Assessment Data Collected: 92% of graduates identified 87% of errors. However, grammatical conventions regarding capitalization were not consistently applied.

_2 a. Use of Results to Improve Instructional Program: Faculty use of commonly accepted conventions regarding capitalization in reviewing upper division papers has been emphasized.

Second Means of Assessment for Outcome Identified Above:

___ b. Means of Program Assessment & Criteria for Success:

___ b. Summary of Assessment Data Collected:

___ b. Use of Results to Improve Instructional Program:

Form C

ASSESSMENT REPORT
FOR

English Program

(Instructional Degree Program)

Bachelor of Arts

(Degree Level)

September 2000-August 2001

(Period Covered)

September 15, 2001

(Date Submitted)

Intended Educational (Student) Outcome:

NOTE: There should be one form C for each intended outcome listed on form B. Intended outcome should be restated in the box immediately below and the intended outcome number entered in the blank spaces.

3. Students completing the baccalaureate program will be capable of writing an acceptable journal article.

First Means of Assessment for Outcome Identified Above:

_3 a. Means of Program Assessment & Criteria for Success: A jury of English dept. faculty from an institution comparable to Our University will judge 80% of those journal articles submitted acceptable for publication.

_3 a. Summary of Assessment Data Collected: 55% of articles reviewed were found acceptable for publication.

_3 a. Use of Results to Improve Instructional Program: English 407 (advanced writing) is being modified to include journal article exercise.

Second means of Assessment for Outcome Identified Above:

_3 b. Means of Assessment & Criteria for Success: 20% of journal articles submitted will be published in student or other publications.

_3 b. Summary of Assessment Data Collected: 10% of articles were published.

_3 b. Use of Results to Improve Instructional Program: Additional outlets for student publishing are being explored.

Form C

NOTES